Accredited Investor CrowdFunding: A Practical Guide For Technology CEOs and Entrepreneurs

Laurie Thomas Vass

The Great American Business & Economics Press
GABBY Press

Printed in the United States of America
January 2017

3rd Edition ISBN: 978-0-9794388-5-1

D1523968

Table of Contents

Schedule of Diagrams in Accredited Investor CrowdFunding

Introduction to Accredited Investor CrowdFunding

It actually sets yeoman farmers, too poor as individuals to provide even so much as a single share of capital, to combining into groups of a dozen or more for the purpose; it sets laborers to forming pools into which each man pays as little as twenty-five cents per week.

W. J. Cash, in The Mind of the South, describing the origins of equity CrowdFunding of the Southern textile industry in North Carolina.

At a 2013 CrowdFunding presentation in Wilmington, N. C., a representative of IndieGoGo, a charitable giving crowdfunding website, used the historical reference of the funding for the Statue of Liberty as an early example of donor-based CrowdFunding.

She noted that Joseph Pulitzer had started a drive for donations to complete the project that attracted more than 120,000 contributors, most of whom gave less than a dollar. Pulitzer, publisher of the World, a New York newspaper, announced a drive to raise $100,000, and pledged to print the name of every contributor in his newspaper, no matter how small the amount given.

Pulitzer began publishing the notes he received from contributors. He wrote that" a young girl alone in the world" donated "60 cents, the result of self denial." He noted that one donor gave "five cents as a poor office boy's mite toward the Pedestal Fund." A group of children sent a dollar as "the money we saved to go to the circus with."

Fundraising for the Statue of Liberty began in 1882, and is a good historical example of one type of CrowdFunding, categorized as donor, or charitable giving, by CrowdSourcing.org, a global website for CrowdFunding. (Note to readers: CrowdSourcing is no longer in business).

In the case of charitable giving, the donor does not expect a profit, but derives some satisfaction from contributing to a cause that the donor believes in.

Another category of CrowdFunding is called "equity" CrowdFunding. A good historical example of equity CrowdFunding is the North Carolina Farmer's Alliance, beginning around 1885. As described by W. J. Cash, in *The Mind of the South*, (New York: Alfred A. Knopf, 1941), farmers contributed cash to build local textile mills, based upon an expectation of future profit.

Cash captured wildfire enthusiasm of the farmers in Southern communities who were engaged in CrowdFunding capital for community economic development projects. "The impulse leaps from community to community, Cash wrote, "as an electric current leaps across a series of galvanic poles—sweeping the citizens into mass assembly. . . . It actually sets yeoman farmers, too poor as individuals to provide even so much as a single share of capital, to combining into groups of a dozen or more for the purpose; it sets laborers to forming pools into which each man pays as little as twenty-five cents per week."

As Dwight Billings, in *The Making of the New South*, noted, "A relationship grew up between the communities and their mills that was and has remained unique in an industrial region. The communities built the mills, and the mills saved the communities. The mills 'belonged' to the communities."

In donor based CrowdFunding, the source of capital, and the profit from the donation, does not matter to the donor, because there is not going to be a second round of capital investment in the project. In other words, after the Statute of Liberty got placed on its pedestal, the initial source of capital did not need to generate profits for the donor.

The same analysis can be applied to the period of time after a venture capital investment has been made. If the intial round of venture capital results in the capital gain exit, the profits are generally not going to be reinvested back into the enterprise. The venture capitalist will generally look for the next most promising startup or new venture.

In equity CrowdFunding, also known as "accredited investor crowdfunding," there is both an expectation of future profit, and a likelihood that the investors will continue to support the enterprise over an extended period of time.

A second distinction between accredited investor CrowdFunding and venture capital investments concerns the stage of growth of the target enterprise. Accredited investor CrowdFunding falls into a much bigger category called private placements.

The great majority of the total $800 billion invested in all Reg D private placements in 2012, was made in established companies that needed small amounts of capital to
grow.

In contrast, the great majority of investments made by venture capitalists and angel partnerships are in early stage, or new ventures. The expectation for the venture capitalist investor is for a very large capital gain, taken within a short period of time.

The purpose of this book is to describe how an established technology company or commercial real estate partnership can use CrowdFunding to raise capital from accredited investors.

The book is targeted to small private technology companies, usually with less than 10 employees, and with more than 3 years of operational experience.

The book is also intended for executives and partners of commercial real estate firms who desire to raise large amounts of capital, at one time, to fund large scale developments. Generally, for commercial real estate firms, the amount of the capital raise would be over $10 million.

Generally, for technology companies, the goal for the amount raised would be around $1 - 3 million. Most of the capital would be used for such items as new staff, sales and marketing, and new capital equipment. From a technological point of view, the capital would generally be used to improve an existing product or service, called a sustaining innovation.

The target market for finding potential investors for both technology firms and commercial real estate partnerships is the 8 million, or so, wealthy individuals, who earn more than $200,000 per year. These type of wealthy investors are commonly called "accredited" because they meet the criteria and guidelines in SEC rules for making a risky private investment.

Research on the location of the majority of the 150,000 accredited investors who actually make private capital investments, indicate that they live within 50 miles of the firm that is raising capital.

Generally, according to rulings made by the U. S. Supreme Court, these type of accredited investors are assumed to be able to "fend for themselves" in making a decision to invest. Each company that is using accredited investor CrowdFunding would not expect to find, or need more than 10 or 15 investors, who are able to fend for themselves, and who would have some predisposition to understand the merits of the investment.

This book is not about donor-based CrowdFunding, or its near cousin, non-accredited investor CrowdFunding, authorized under Title III of the 2012 JOBS Act.

This book is intended for CEOs of technology companies and real estate executives who would like to learn more about this new technique of raising capital.

Diagram 1 compares the older venture capital method to the newer Reg D 506c method of raising capital.

Diagram 1.

Comparison of Old Venture Capital Model to New Accredited Investor Crowdfunding Model of Raising Capital.
The Private Capital Market, Inc. © March 2016.

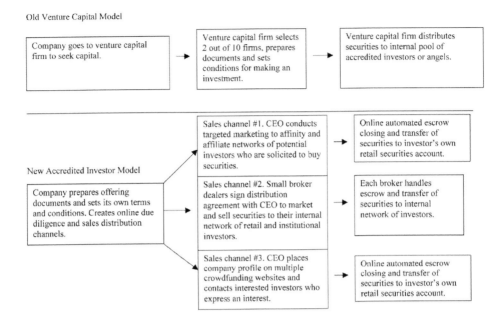

Old Venture Capital Model

| Company goes to venture capital firm to seek capital. | → | Venture capital firm selects 2 out of 10 firms, prepares documents and sets conditions for making an investment. | → | Venture capital firm distributes securities to internal pool of accredited investors or angels. |

New Accredited Investor Model

Company prepares offering documents and sets its own terms and conditions. Creates online due diligence and sales distribution channels.

Sales channel #1. CEO conducts targeted marketing to affinity and affiliate networks of potential investors who are solicited to buy securities.

Online automated escrow closing and transfer of securities to investor's own retail securities account.

Sales channel #2. Small broker dealers sign distribution agreement with CEO to market and sell securities to their internal network of retail and institutional investors.

Each broker handles escrow and transfer of securities to internal network of investors.

Sales channel #3. CEO places company profile on multiple crowdfunding websites and contacts interested investors who express an interest.

Online automated escrow closing and transfer of securities to investor's own retail securities account.

Chapter I. Understanding The Benefits of A Reg D Rule 506(c) Private Offering

One way to gain an understanding of the benefits of accredited investor crowdfunding is to begin the analysis by seeing the investment from the perspective of a potential investor.

Imagining how the investor views private investment opportunities, compared to all other investment alternatives, is useful because it provides an insight into how investors may select either a crowdfunding website or a direct corporate private offering to complete their investment decision in a private offering.

Imagining the investment from the perspective of the investor is also an essential mental exercise for all CEOs who are contemplating raising capital via a Reg D Rule 506(c) offering. The new SEC rules authorize the CEO to market the securities, on behalf of the company, and part of the successful raise requires that CEOs become the best securities salesperson the company has ever seen.

Private securities are sold, not bought. And, the CEO is the person legally responsible for selling the securities.

This insight means that the CEO, and any other designated officer of the company, must do the hard work to sell the securities during the offering period. Part of the benefit of using a crowdfunding website is that websites offer promotional services that make selling and marketing of private securities easier for the CEO.

CEOs may need that help from websites because of the market gap between the sales of private securities and public securities. The marketing infrastructure for selling public securities is well established, and serviced by about 650,000 stock brokers.
Given the stock of the day, the brokers pick up the phone, and call customers to sell the stocks.

In comparison, there is nothing like this professional sales market infrastructure for selling private securities. The private placement broker dealer community, based upon a February 2016 survey of FINRA broker dealers, indicates that there are less than 100 broker firms in the U. S. who conduct the sales of private placements, under Reg D Rule 506(c).

Crowdfunding websites are filling part of the gap in selling and distributing private securities caused by the absence of broker dealer sales agents in the private capital markets.

At the very beginning of the analysis of how to sell private securities, CEOs must decide the right path of distribution between using a website, or conducting a direct corporate private offering, (DCPO).

The reason this subtle distinction about investor perspectives is important, especially to CEOs, is that engaging in the private placement process, either on a website, or direct, implies a shift in their daily management activities. It is a rough estimate that during the six month offering period, the CEO could be spending about 60% of her daily management tasks attempting to sell the securities.

When an investor begins the search for suitable investment opportunities, they generally have some rules-of-thumb about the relationship between risk and potential future return on the investment. They generally will use those informal rules to compare broad asset categories, such as public stocks compared to corporate bonds, or private equity versus an investment in commercial real estate.

They have some existing knowledge about the customary, usual returns for example of commercial real estate because they have seen investment performance reports on the internet, or they have heard their business associates describe their experience. They use this past experience to imagine how the investment would fit into their goals.

The fancy economic idea here is that investors have a mental image of their own welfare, and are always in the process of comparing investments according to how the investment fits into their "welfare" function. The human brain is always engaged in a furious search for the path that optimizes welfare, and making an investment decision involves the brain searching and sorting thousands of images, trying to come up with the right solution.

The range of investment returns, which is only one of several criteria that the investor's brain is sorting would be along the following lines:

For an equity/ownership interest in a 5 year old technology company, generally in the form of preferred stock, the criteria for returns would be around 18% - 22% per year. For commercial real estate investments, the expected return would be lower, the common rule-of-thumb return would be between 11% to 13%.

Most accredited investors do not make very sophisticated calculations about returns. What the investor expects to make, in either technology or real estate, is a total return of around 13%. In both types of investments, the investor would generally look to exit the investment within 3 to 5 years.

For corporate bonds, the investor generally has in mind a return of around 8% to 10% interest rate per year.

For longer term private 10-year senior debt, the investor expects around 7%.

The investor will generally compare their assumptions and expectations about non-real estate investments with real estate, because real estate is so widely held by investors.

For example, investors are aware that CDs and money market returns are around 1%. They have read sensationalized media accounts that venture capital returns are around 800%. They have read reports that the biggest S & P 500 stocks have a historic annualized return of around 10%.

The point for CEOs is to see and imagine what the investor is thinking about in selecting an investment category, and see the world from the eyes of investors, beginning with these rules-of-thumb on returns. If the firm is not able to compete with the returns in the other asset classes, then there is no logic in trying to raise capital.

But, returns are only part of the calculation the brain of the investor is making. The biggest factor for investors making the choice of asset category is fear of losing their investment capital, which is called market risk.

For example, data from the National Council of Real Estate Investment Fiduciaries suggests that private commercial real estate investments returned an 8.4% average return between 2000 and 2010. The average return in the stock market, for the S&P 500, over that same period was 1.58%.

Tempering the expected returns in real estate is the experience real estate investors had in the bubble crash of 2008. Many of the real estate investors lost all of their capital in that crash, as did the sock market investors who invested in mortgage backed securities.

Investors know that the 1.58% on stocks in that 10 year period indicates great price volatility and greater risk compared to the 50-year historic return of around 10% on stocks. They also know that both stock investments and real estate investments are subject to panics and price speculation.

The NCREIF Property Index (NPI), which tracks 6,971 investment-grade, income-producing real estate properties in the U.S., of 8.4%, can be compared to the investment return of the Barclays Capital Government Bond Index of 3.99%.

Generally, government bonds have been seen by investors as being safer than either stocks or commercial real estate. Investors do not generally assume that the government bonds will default or crash.

Investors will generally use the government bond returns as the lower range of potential investments, and then go through a process of adjusting the risk to come up with an investment that provides the right "risk adjusted return" for their own unique mental welfare function.

In other words, the investor's mental process is to compare the 3.8% return on government bonds with the 8% potential return in real estate, and the possible 13% return in the more risky equity investments. Using these rule-of-thumb returns as guideposts, investors then begin the process of adjusting the potential higher returns by adding factors which lowers the risk of investing in commercial real estate or non-real estate investments.

One important risk adjustment investors make for real estate concerns what happens if the investment fails or goes bankrupt. Investors are generally aware that an investment in real estate is secured by a lien on the property. They know that in the case of non-payment by the borrower, the investors may initiate legal action to take possession of the collateral secured by the lien to recover their investment.

This type of added security allows the investor to have more confidence about making an investment in real estate, compared to an investment in stocks. So, along the risk adjustment mental calculation being made by the investor, the added security allows them to move the investment up the chain a little bit in order to obtain the higher return.

They also know that if the underlying real estate property goes belly-up that the liquidation proceedings would give them priority over other investors in reclaiming their initial investment. While the investor may not fully understand all the legal nuances of "senior" debt in a court-ordered bankruptcy, they generally are aware that senior debt will be first in line for obtaining any value in the bankruptcy sale of the property.

This additional risk adjustment, known as the "preference," allows the investor to move the real estate investment farther up the risk/reward continuum, starting from the 3.8% return of government bonds.

Investors have also seen the term "preference" used in conjunction with real estate investments, and again, without any great statistical precision, investors know that the term "preference" generally means that they will have less risk in getting interest payments on their investments.

Finally, the last risk adjustment that investors make regards any legal guarantee made by the real estate firm or the other outside firms, that the interest and dividend payments will be made by some outside third party if the parent real estate firm does not make the payments.

The investors generally realize that the guarantee is only as good as the credibility of the outside third party, but knowing that there is a guarantee on getting paid allows the investor to move the real estate investment up the ladder from 3.8%, in hopes of actually obtaining the "hoped-for" return of around 8%.

The main point for CEOs in selling private securities is to emphasize these risk reducing factors of their own particular investment, knowing that the brain of the investor already has a pre-existing mental image about reducing risk in the searching and sorting process.

As a note of regulatory caution, each and every statement or representation about risk that a CEO may contemplate, must be factually accurate and truthful, not omitting any relevant detail that may be used by an investor in the decision-making process.

This pre-existing mental factor of investors means that some of the terms that CEOs of real estate firms currently use to sell securities, for example, like "cap rate," or internal rate of return, will not be as effective in describing an investment as the risk reducing terms, because investors do not have cap rate or IRR on the top of their brain's searching and sorting process.

Telling a potential investor that the cap rate of one property is 5%, and an alternative investment property has a cap rate of 8% is marginally useful information to the investor. Cap rate is generally not a dominant factor in optimizing the welfare function of the brain, while risk is definitely up there in the brain's searching and sorting of images.

The choice being made by investors is one between the very safe return of 3.8% of government bonds and the higher return of 8.4% of commercial real estate, and the even riskier return in technology companies. In the mental calculations of a potential investor, when the 3.8% of government bonds is equivalent to the risk-adjusted return of 8.4% of real estate, the rational investor selects real estate.

The term used by economists to describe this condition is to say that the investor would be indifferent between the government bonds and commercial real estate.

Once the investor calculates the rate of indifference between investment alternatives, the investor begins looking for the least-costly, least painful, process to make the investment, which is where the perspective of the CEO becomes relevant in selecting the method of selling the securities.

CEOs and real estate professionals usually begin their analysis of how to sell their securities by trying to figure out:
- How to put as little of their own capital into the deal as possible,
- How to receive the same preferred return as investors on the firm's own invested capital in the deal,
- How to structure the deal to receive a "promote" (carry) share of the remaining cash flow and profits,
- How to receive some share of the tax benefits related to the deal.

In other words, cap rate and IRR are important terms to the CEO of the real estate firm, and understandably, these are the terms that CEOs use with each other, and with commercial banks, to discuss deals. It is a mistake for the CEOs to attempt to sell private securities by assuming that these same terms are important to the mental images being sorted by potential investors.

Many real estate crowdfunding websites have extended this error made by real estate CEOs by transferring the terms to their own description of the merits of the real estate deals on their websites. The terms have relevance to the bigger, institutional investors, but are not generally relevant to the 8 million investors who meet the criteria of an accredited investor.

Selling securities to the larger institutional investors may be lucrative, as the recent decision by Fundrise to exit crowdfunding in favor of promoting their own version of REITs demonstrates, but selling to institutional investors is not exactly accredited investor crowdfunding.

In other words, to penetrate the vast universe of crowdfunding accredited investors, both CEOs and real estate "crowdfunding" websites need to emphasize the investments from the perspective of the potential investor, and not from the perspective of what benefits the CEO of the real estate firm.

In putting together the terms and conditions of a Reg D Rule 506(c), the task of the CEO is to structure the terms and conditions of their deal that serves the interests of potential investors, while also quietly meeting their own financial interests.

One of the advantages of a direct corporate private offering over the conventional venture capital methods of raising capital is the company's ability to control the terms and conditions of the offering. By creating the documents related to the offering in advance of the offering period, the company CEO avoids the costs and time lost in frustrating negotiations with multiple sources of venture capital, all of who may want to impose their own terms and conditions.

The benefits of the company controlling the terms and conditions must be tempered by two key considerations. First, the terms and conditions must be attractive to a wide range of accredited investors, based upon the merits of the investment itself. In other words, the terms must be fair to the investors so that they may enjoy the benefits associated with making the investment.

In the 506c offering, the investors are not going to have an opportunity to negotiate over the terms and conditions of their private securities, so the terms initially established by the CEO must be fair for them from the start.

Second, the terms and conditions for the company in the early rounds of capital must be compatible with future rounds. This means that a logical sequence of terms and conditions must flow through all of the eventual rounds of capital raising.

The priority for the company CEO in the creation of the documents must be that they are created right and fairly from the beginning and then continue to be fair for future investors, throughout the life of the company.

The company CEO will need to work with legal counsel to get the exact form and text of the terms and conditions to fit the type of securities for the specific offering today and in the future.

The first consideration for the CEO in contemplating a private placement is the type of security for the business to issue to investors. Most companies that have some capital gain potential, as opposed to an investor's interest in the dividend income potential from stable revenues, issue preferred stock.

Preferred stock has various "preferences" over common stock. These preferences can include liquidation preferences, dividend rights, redemption rights, conversion rights and voting rights, as described in more detail below. The "preferences" in preferred stock are also called terms and conditions.

For real estate investments, the preferences are combined with the safety factors of third-party guarantees on the investment.

The text for the conditions attach to both the security itself, and to other elements associated with the investment. The same terms, such as "participating," may be used for different parts of the investment. For example, "participating" can apply to both participating in the flow dividends and to participating in the profits at liquidation.

When used in different elements of the investment, the preferences tend to compound the original, single use of the term "preference." The preferences associated with preferred stock allows the investor to benefit from a capital gain event because the stock represents equity in the company, and as the value of the equity goes up, the investors can obtain the larger gain when the stock is sold.

Venture capitalists and other investors in the older model typically receive preferred stock for their investment. Most of the negotiations in raising capital in the conventional method, where the company goes searching for capital at individual venture capital sources, concern the priorities and rights for the "preferences" between the investors and the company.

All of the good features and rights associated with the self-underwriting of preferred stock can be used to provide investors with greater security and reduced risk of loss of capital, while the more onerous features regarding venture capital control over decision making authority, can be eliminated.

An additional benefit for investors and the company in a 506c direct corporate private offering (DCPO), is that standardization across many different companies, all of whom issued stock with common terms and conditions, would eventually lead to easier transactions in the future via private securities exchanges.

Common terms and conditions would lead to greater liquidity in the private capital marketplace because less time and expense would be involved in determining how one security's rights and features differed from another security.

One of the important features and rights associated with preferred stock is its ability to be issued with conversion rights into common stock at some point in the future.

In the older method, the convertible preferred stock contained onerous anti-dilution protection for investors in the event that a second round of securities is issued to new investors at lower prices than the earlier rounds.

In the conventional venture capital model, the earlier investors had a built-in conflict of financial interest with the company associated with their capital costs of owning the stock. If the value of the company dropped, or the company did not meet the metrics of performance imposed by the capitalists, the conversion rights allowed the earlier investors to obtain a bigger profit when the stock was eventually sold, or the company itself was sold, for a gain.

As the name suggests, convertible preferred stock can also convert into common stock at either the holder's option or at the option of the company. Usually, there is some form of coerced or mandatory conversion feature for all investors if the company becomes involved in an Initial Public Offering (IPO), or company buy-out, where all the private stock is converted to publicly-traded stock.

Some of the onerous features in the older method of this form of equity, from the company's and founder's perspective, is that the earlier rights provide for a guaranteed return of capital through redemption provisions if the company's performance is mediocre. This explains one of the reasons why such a high percentage of companies in the earlier method were terminated by the capitalists if the company did not meet performance metrics.

In the earlier method, the investors were going to obtain a profit no matter what happened to the company.

These more onerous features of conversion upon redemption do not have to be inserted in a 506c company self-underwriting.

Convertible preferred stock often pays or agrees to pay some form of dividends, which can be paid in cash, or in the form of deferred additional shares. Usually the dividend rate is set by a vote of the Board of Directors. In the older model, one of the terms set by the investors was control over the Board of Directors, who could vote for dividends and also had the power to fire or terminate the original founders and entrepreneurs.

The payment of dividends is very beneficial to investors, as it gives them two ways to benefit from owning company stock. First, they may obtain a capital gain profit when they sell their stock, and second, they may also be paid income during the period of time they are waiting for the value of their stock to go up in price.

This type of outside investor control by the Board of Directors, so prevalent in the earlier model, can be avoided in the self-underwriting.

The burden of making the self underwritten private offering attractive to investors from the beginning means that the company and its legal counsel will need to carefully balance provisions that shareholders would find attractive with provisions that are fair to the company.

Since the direct corporate private self underwriting process does not involve negotiations like the older model, the initial set of provisions needs to be attractive to both the investors and the company right from the start.

Among the important considerations of additional protective provisions are:

- A majority vote of the outstanding preferred stock holders to make any amendment or changes to the rights, preferences, privileges, or powers of, or the restrictions provided for the benefit of, the preferred stock;
- A majority vote of the outstanding preferred stock holders to authorize any increases or decreases in the authorized number of shares of Common or Preferred stock;
- A majority vote of the outstanding preferred stock holders any action that authorizes, creates, or issues shares of any class of stock having senior rights or preferences over existing shareholders;
- The broadest possible information rights and inspection rights possible with greater rights attached to owners of at least 15% of the total outstanding preferred stock.

In conformity with the provisions of Sarbanes-Oxley on public companies, private companies should aim at transparency and truthful dealings with their shareholders.

Documents such as audited annual and GAAP unaudited quarterly financial statements, annual budgets and monthly financial statements, minutes of the meetings of the Board should be made available to preferred shareholders in pass word protected areas of the company's investor relations web page.

The major desired outcome of raising growth capital, from the perspective of the company, is to obtain capital that helps the company grow. With the 506c direct corporate private offering, companies gain more control over their destiny when they seek growth capital.

Part of the solution for small companies gaining control over their destiny is to offer the securities directly to investors in a private placement self underwriting, always mindful of the fact that the prosperity that results from the company's successful growth must be distributed fairly to all those who took the risk to invest.

For real estate investments, there are many benefits related to creating the Special Purpose Entity (SPE), to issue the securities, but the biggest reason to begin the private placement process with the SPE is that investors like the idea of investing in a "bankrupt-proof" entity.

The sequence and logic of events in conducting a Reg D Rule 506(c) for a real estate firm is to get the legal SPE structure in place first. This implies that all of the factors that investors use to adjust risk must be incorporated into the legal documents that create the SPE, and then to display the risk factors prominently in the risk disclosure document that is provided to potential investors.

These risk reducing legal terms are:
- Establishing the seniority of the securities,
- Establishing the preferences of the securities,
- Establishing the liens and trustee arrangements in the transfer of the titles to the SPE,
- Establishing the guarantees for payment of dividends and interest.

Using a real estate crowdfunding website to distribute the securities transfers some of these tasks to the website, which usually has standardized legal templates for all of these terms and conditions. The real estate crowdfunding website becomes the "issuer" of the securities, and creates its own SPE to issue the securities on behalf of the real estate company.

Part of the complexity of issuing 506(c) securities in a direct corporate private offering, seen from the perspective of the real estate CEO, is that they must conduct their own internal self-initiated due diligence on the offering, before investors ever see any part of the offering.

The chronology of events involved in the offering process does not allow for back-and-forth negotiations between the investors and the company, and once the CEO begins the public promotion of the securities, the offering documents must be perfect.

This is a very different set of conditions than the traditional 506(b) process that allows for ongoing private negotiations between investors and the company.

At the very front end of the offering process, the CEO must do two important tasks, from the company's own financial perspective, that involves the creation of the SPE.

They must determine the mix of securities the SPE will issue, based upon the estimate of what the potential investor is most likely to buy, knowing in advance that the investors generally understand 3 types of securities:

- Long-term senior debt, that looks like commercial backed mortgages.
- Convertible bonds, that looks like mezzanine debt.
- Preferred stock, that looks like joint venture equity.

They must determine the mix of real estate assets to place into the SPE, knowing in advance that the properties must be revenue-producing, high-quality cash flowing properties.

In other words, the CEO must first examine the company's own set of real estate properties and financial condition, and then structure the deal to match the investment opportunity to both the goals of the CEO and to potential investors.

After this initial set of legal tasks has been completed, the CEO must engage a securities attorney to prepare the offering documents that the SPE will issue. The attorney who drafts the SPE will probably not be the same attorney who prepares the security offering documents. These two legal tasks involve different legal skills and very few legal professionals combine the two skill sets.

One of the big difference between a real estate crowdfunding website and the direct corporate private offering method is that the websites generally will have template legal forms for all of the offering documents.

In this case, the CEO will not have to retain a securities attorney, in favor of using the website's legal offering documents.

What the CEO in both real estate and technology firms gain in ease of issuance and lower costs with the websites is lost in terms of flexibility for structuring a deal that meets the financial goals of the company. The templates of the website are generally uniform and standardized documents, and the range of securities for each website SPE is very limited.

Part of the flexibility benefit of the direct private placement offering, not using a website, is that it allows the company to put less of its own capital in the deal, compared to either a bank or a crowdfunding website.

Most bank lenders today require a developer to invest cash equity to cover 25-40% of the total project cost.

Most websites are asking the CEO for around 20% of the total capital to be invested in the SPE. The other 80% is usually in the form of debt, for a debt-to-value ratio that looks just like the ones favored by a commercial banker.

Generally, the SPE method allows the company to put about 10% capital into the deal, and to issue about 60% of the total value in senior long term debt, with the rest of the capital being raised in a combination of convertible bonds and preferred stock.

As a matter of comparison, much of what the real estate websites have done is borrow the revenue model of commercial bankers, and have applied that model to their online business model.

Part of the benefit of flexibility in the SPE method is that it overcomes a barrier for subordinated debt, generally used for short term financing to get the deal organized. In 2009, national credit rating agencies such as Standard & Poor's and Moody's required that bank-originated commercial mortgage backed securities (CMBS), not include any mortgage loan that also involved a subordinated mortgage debt on the property.

The SPE adds back into the mix the type of mezzanine funding that helps get the real estate project off the ground.

Another benefit of the flexibility of the SPE for the company is that the SPE tends to have the appearance of a REIT, but without the drawbacks for investors of the blind-pool REIT characteristics. A REIT is essentially a corporation that owns and manages a portfolio of income-producing real estate properties such as apartments, hotels, malls and office buildings.

The drawback for investors is that the REITs generally do not disclose, in advance, the properties that make up the REIT. In contrast, the SPE allows the investor to see exactly the properties that comprise the investment, before and after making an investment in the properties of the SPE. Seeing the properties, and being able to go by and "kick-the-tires" after the offering, tends to reduce the level of risk for the investor.

The CEO is free to mix and match the real estate properties for each SPE to suit the company's financial needs, while providing potential investors with the greatest transparency in advance of making an investment. This transparency tends to reduce the risk for the investor of making a bad investment decision.

REITs are very lucrative for the investment management company, and as noted above, one of the best real estate crowdfunding websites, Fundrise, gave up entirely the crowdfunding part of its business model to convert its model to the issuance of REITs.

The same logic used by Fundrise to make its decision to exit crowdfunding can easily be adopted by real estate CEOs by structuring their offering with the characteristics of an investor-friendly REIT.

The CEO can use the SPE to create a very large deal with multiple properties that looks like a REIT, up to at least $50 million, and then sell the investment units to accredited investors in much smaller units.

The data from real estate crowdfunding websites is that the average real estate investment being made by accredited investors is around $50,000 in a single real estate deal.

From the perspective of the CEO contemplating this model, it is much easier to sell a $20 million deal in bite-sized units of $50,000, than it is to sell the project to one big investor for $20 million.

Fees and costs can be seen from the perspective of the investor, who begins their analysis with the risk adjustment mental process, and then searches for the least costly, least painful method of making the investment, or from the perspective of the company that is issuing the securities.

Some websites charge a fee to both investors and the company, some just charge a fee to the company for the initial service, and some charge the company on-going fees for as long as the offering remains active.

For example, Fundrise charged 3% of any lease in the SPE, 1% for asset management for all properties in the SPE, 1% for financing origination, as well as development fees. For investors, these fees meant about a loss of potential return of about 14% right off the top.

Companies and CEOs do not generally go through the "risk adjustment" process the same way that investors do. CEOs begin the process by trying to figure out how to make the most money at the least cost. The time horizon for making money is generally set by when the property will be sold or re-financed, which is usually 5 – 7 years.

Generally, CEOs break up fees and costs into two broad categories, those costs that must be paid upfront, out-of-pocket, and those costs that can be put off until some future time,

For example, brokers, and some attorneys will defer collecting fees until the closing event, much like a traditional residential real estate closing where all the vendors and attorneys get paid.

CEOs tend to prefer costs that can be put off until the future. With this beginning classification of costs, it is easier to begin with the costs, to the company, of issuing securities in a direct corporate Reg D Rule 506(c) offering.

Legal fees to create the Special Purpose Entity upfront		$5,000
Legal fees to create the offering documents	upfront	$15,000
Legal fees to re-title property to the SPE upfront		$5,000
Required capital from CEO upfront		10% of capital
Marketing and sales to sell securities	over 6 months	$20,000
Fees to websites to certify investors	over 6 months	$2000
Fees to websites for online escrow	day of closing	1% of capital
Fees (optional) to brokers to sell securities	day of closing	8% of capital
Fees (optional) to investment advisor	day of closing	3% of capital
Fees to manage investments of SPE	after closing	1% of capital

These fees and out-of-pocket do not include the costs in time for the CEO to go out and market and sell the securities for a period of 6 months. The CEO will need to go out and give speeches, get on the radio and television to describe the offering, go to angel and capital market events, and pick up the telephone to call prospective investors, just like a stock broker does.

During the offering period, the CEO will likely spend about 20 hours per week in sales and marketing activities. Economists call these type of costs "opportunity" costs for the lost opportunities that the CEO endures in selling securities, rather than managing the company.

To compare these "opportunity" costs of a direct corporate private offering, there is an opportunity cost of using a website to issue the securities. The opportunity cost of the website is the cost of lost flexibility and future opportunities "foregone" because the website forecloses future opportunities for the CEO to use the real estate properties, once the titles are transferred to the website SPE.

As mentioned above, there is no uniformity in the fees imposed by the broker dealer intermediary websites, and the disclosure of fees by the websites is splotchy, at best.

Fees to conduct the initial due diligence on the company by the broker

- upfront and deferred $10,000
- Required capital by CEO   upfront   20%
- Fees to brokers to sell securitiesday of closing   8% of capital
- Fees for online escrow day of closing   1% of capital
- Ongoing annual management fees after closing   1% of capital
- Cost of loan origination on debt day of closing   3% of capital

Seeing the investing decision from the eyes of a potential accredited investor is beneficial to the CEO because that perspective provides an insight into how investors may select between a real estate investment or a non-real estate direct corporate private offering.

At the point of making an investment, the investor is searching for the least costly, least painful method of investing. In many respects, the broker dealer intermediary websites have boiled this process for the investor down to a painless process.

For CEOs who need a comprehensive, packaged solution for raising capital, accredited investor websites are the best choice because the CEO transfers many of the legal and administrative tasks to the website. Some of the websites offer a cost solution that is very reasonable for this type of deal and for the services provided by the website.

Even with the services of the website, the CEO must still become the best securities sales person the company has ever seen because even with the help of selling the securities of the broker dealer website, the CEO must spend time promoting the deal.

This task means picking up the telephone and calling potential investors to sell them on the merits of the deal, and then directing them to the real estate investor relations website, and from there to the outside website, where they conduct the exchange.

For more complicated deals that require more strategy, the 506c direct corporate private offering is a better choice for the CEO than using a website. The reason is that the CEO can match their own terms and conditions to meet the needs of potential investors, while still meeting their own needs for raising capital.

The best benefit for the CEO of the Reg D Rule 506(c) offering is putting together deals for investors in their home communities, and helping the local community of investors achieve greater prosperity through their investments in real estate deals, that would otherwise been out of their reach. Once the CEOs learn how to do this private offering, they will do it over and over again, and their pool of investors will continue to grow.

Chapter 2. A Brief History Of Crowdfunding

Raising small amounts of capital has been an enduring problem for America's small businesses. The gap in the private capital markets is especially severe for operational high tech companies trying to raise between $150,000 and $5 million.

The problem has been widely recognized by economists and policy makers for at least 100 years, but little progress has been made to overcome the issues confronting this part of the private capital market. In its review of the problem, in 1919, the New York Times noted that larger institutions did not seem interested in providing small amounts of capital to small established firms.

Just like the current venture capital emphasis on startups and new ventures, many years ago, most investors were primarily interested in discovering very early stage companies that had great investment potential.

Small companies that had been operational for several years and needed growth capital to grow were not a high priority for private investors 100 years ago.

"More than ever before in financial history," wrote the New York Times in 1919, "the small investor in the United States may be an important factor in financing business and building." The Times was reporting on a news story about an idea to pool the capital of small investors into a type of "fund" that would have trustees that would direct the capital to small businesses.

They concluded their story by suggesting that a market mechanism needed to be created that allowed small companies to easily meet small investors. Citing the US Department of Labor, the article stated: "It is essential, in the opinion of the Department of Labor, to devise ways and means of availing of the small investors' capital."

As categorized by the global website Crowdsourcing.org, (currently out of business), there are currently about 2500 internet websites that "avail" themselves to crowdfunding capital for small companies.

The websites provide a new type of market mechanism that brings small companies together with investors, much like the suggestion made in 1919 by the New York Times.

The great majority of websites tracked by Crowdsourcing.org fall into a category for donor-based or charitable giving, like Indiegogo. In the charitable giving website model, the donor gives a gift to the company, or the social political cause, without any expectation of future return on the gift.

Another very large category of crowdfunding websites fall into the category of very early stage entrepreneurial companies. The early stage Crowdsourcing category of websites includes both the donor-based model, and the equity investment model, where the investor hopes to make large, fast capital gains from the investment.

A subcategory of equity crowdfunding websites are those that are oriented to very early stage companies, who seek to attract investments from non-accredited investors. In this model, the motivation for the websites and the investors is to provide an investment opportunity for non-accredited investors that was previously only available to venture capital firms and angel partnerships.

In other words, in the Crowdsourcing subcategory of websites that promote equity crowdfunding investments, most of the websites target very early, non-operational companies, and try to attract non-accredited investors to make investments in the entrepreneurial companies.

Diagram 2 below is useful for describing the main categories of internet crowdfunding websites that are tracked and categorized by Crowdsourcing.org.

In their use of terminology, the word "crowdsourcing" is a main category, while the word "crowdfunding" is used to describe a subset of all crowdsourcing.

The typical scenario for the matching sites operated by angel investor groups would include having the entrepreneur or firm submit a document for review by the angel group administer, who screened and evaluated the deal.

This process of online screening was just like the process that took place in person, in an earlier era, when the entrepreneur presented a power point presentation to the angel an group or venture capital group, at an event called a venture capital forum.

Statistics compiled by the University of New Hampshire indicated that in 2007, about 1 out of 10 deals submitted to an angel group were actually funded by the angel group.

Diagram 2. Comparison of Websites

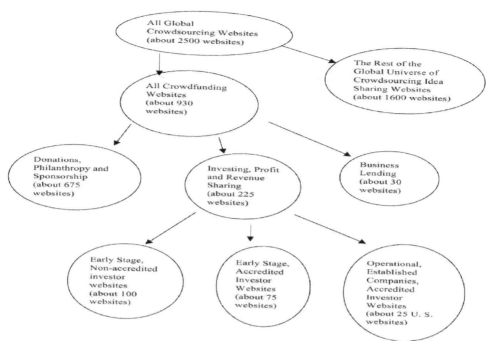

The use of the internet tended to speed up the initial review process for the firm that was trying to raise capital. The value for the firm of submitting to one angel website was that most angel sites used the same standardized format for the initial submission.

After the entrepreneur prepared one document, that same template could be used over and over again because the angel matching websites all accepted the standardized document.

For example, one early matching company, AngelSoft (now called Gust), created both document template software and web portals for the same submission form to be submitted by the entrepreneur to many different angel groups. At one time, AngelSoft was submitting the same proposal to an angel membership list of about 500 angel and venture capital firms.

As they noted on their website, "Since 2004, Angelsoft has been building tools to help Startups and Investors communicate more effectively. Today, 446 Angel Groups and VCs, 16,735 Angel Investors, and 3,500 new entrepreneurs a month use our tools to take the first step toward building the best new companies of the 21st Century." (www.angelsoft.net).

In contrast to the angel matching websites, an alternative internet website model to raise capital was an open platform, like GoBig. They stated on their website that, "The Go BIG Network is an on-line marketplace that connects the startup and small business community. The company allows startup companies, funding sources, advisors, and service providers to post requests for help on-line and have those requests routed to other members of the Network who can help them." (www.gobignetwork.com).

The more open websites, like GoBig, were like internet private capital marketplaces. The early marketplaces were meeting places on the internet for the 3 parties to a capital exchange, but generally these websites did not offer much functionality for firms and investors to conduct a transaction.

As stated on their website, "members of Go BIG can either search profiles of other members and contact them or they can post a Request (like a classified ad) and let other members see what they are looking for."

To summarize, in the evolution of crowdfunding websites, the early investor matching websites looked and functioned like the early dating websites, like Match.com, where potential partners could search and sort profiles.

A more full service type of angel internet marketplace, with back end website transaction functionality, was NVST.com. NVST is the grand daddy of angel matching websites, and was way ahead of its time, beginning around 1996.

As they note on their website, "NVST since 1996 has been the leading platform for private investment opportunities. The complete solution for the professional investor, advisor and entrepreneur, including market intelligence, deal flow, and intermediary services." (www.nvst.com).

The most important distinction between the earlier versions and the most recent versions of crowdfunding carried over from the traditional angel or venture capital model.

In the newer internet crowdfunding strategy, the company is controlling the terms and conditions of the entire private offering of securities. In the traditional model, the company goes to the capital source, asking for capital, and the angels or VCs control the terms and conditions of the securities that they will buy from the company.

Of the one out of 10 deals initially funded in the traditional model, about three out of 10 make profits for the angels, and only one out of 10 hit the "homerun."

The traditional model focused on very early stage companies that could hit the homerun, while the newer model is based upon companies that can share revenues and growth through consistent sales revenues.

Understanding the crucial distinction at the beginning of the capital raise between the traditional route and the newer internet crowdfunding model means that the company must prepare the entire private offering prior to making a public solicitation for investors.

In the older method, now designated Reg D Rule 506(b), the company usually would go to the angels or venture capital firms, who would set the terms and conditions, and prepare all the offering documents.

Under the older method, there is no reason for the company to engage in sales and marketing to find investors, if the company can find them in the venture capital community.

All securities transactions, even accredited investor private exempt transactions, are subject to the antifraud provisions of the 1933 Securities Act and the myriad of other federal securities laws.

The anti-fraud provisions are the most important reason why any public statements or press releases, under Reg D Rule 506(c), must not contain any form of misleading statement.

From the very first moment of the accredited investor private offering process, the company and the CEO is responsible for false or misleading statements, whether oral or written.

Chapter 3. The Current Political and Legal Status of Accredited Investor CrowdFunding

In order to better understand the current legal and political status of accredited investor CrowdFunding, the best place to start is to understand what the evolution of the internet means to the process of raising capital,

The internet, and the new phenomenon of business social networks, like LinkedIn, provide new channels of communication between the three parties to a capital market exchange.

Investors can use the new networks to discover ideas and possible deals, the companies that need capital can use the internet to allow investors to investigate their company, and the wide variety of third party professional advisors, who act as intermediaries between buyers and sellers of capital can find new clients in the social networks.

Part of the reason why the technological capabilities of the internet have not already solved the age-old problems of small companies who need capital is that the technology innovations of the internet have outpaced the conception of the business model that would be required to take advantage of the technology.

Part of understanding the current story of CrowdFunding is related to the slow development of websites that make money helping companies raise capital. Accredited Investor CrowdFunding has been legal since September 23rd 2013, but as the article in Fortune suggests, it has been very slow to catch on. (Why the Most Significant Part of the JOBS Act Has Yet to Catch On Jeremy Quittner. Updated: Sep 20, 2016).

In other words, the internet technology for facilitating much greater rates of capital investments in small high technology companies already exists. However, like so much about the internet, the business model to make money using the internet to solve capital market problems has not been well-developed.

The recent technology improvements in software coding of websites has also allowed for more communication possibilities in capital market transactions. Most of the newer websites have extensive "behind-the-front door" administrative functions that let the owner of the website make instant changes to the text and also monitor and authorize users to enter pass-word protected portals that are not visible to other users.

MarketWatch, and internet news site, (http://www.marketwatch.com) tracks the daily activity of 18 equity crowdfunding websites, out of a total population of about 35 equity sites, where companies can place a listing to raise capital. Alchemy Global, Crowdfunder, CrowdStreet, DarcMatter, EarlyShares, EquityNet, Jumpstart, MicroVentures, OneVest, OurCrowd, Patch of Land, Prodigy Network, RealCrowd, Realty Mogul, Seed Equity, SeedInvest truCrowd, Wefunder.

Many of the different websites are linked and connected to each other by new social media outlets like Digg and Twitter.Often, a company will place the listing on more than one of the websites.

Plus, the newer websites can be enhanced with stand-alone blogs, that function like an independent public relations website for companies to describe what is happening, on a daily, or in the case of Twitter, a minute-by-minute basis.

Part of the solution for using the capabilities of the internet to make money involves a new philosophy, or new way of seeing the possibilities of the internet in an entirely new way. Greek philosophers called this new vision the "telos" or end goal to which the idea is directed. Accredited investor CrowdFunding is a new way to see the internet in its function of raising capital.

The end goal for using the internet for solving the problems of small companies who need capital is to conceive of the internet as an interactive capital marketplace, and not continue to see it as a unidirectional communication medium between buyers and sellers.

Just like the supply chain management software companies, like MIE Solutions (http://www.mie-solutions.com/mie/), who use the internet as a market exchange for facilitating bidding and quoting between vendors and customers in specific industrial sectors, the same idea could easily be applied to a more ubiquitous geographical marketplace, for transactions between buyers and sellers of private capital.

Like so many other markets, like a local flea market, or local farmer's market, or the earlier example of early New York Stock Exchange, the internet is the market place where the three parties to the exchange meet each other. In the examples of the earlier markets, the meeting place was a physical location in a distinct geographical setting, such as meeting under the trees on Wall Street where the early stock traders met.

CrowdFunding can be seen as a new type of internet marketplace. Imagining the internet as a capital market would mean combining the existing technological capabilities into a web-based business model that functioned like the older marketplaces. The three parties to a capital market exchange could meet each other online to communicate and share knowledge about doing possible deals.

The internet can be used as the platform to help companies raise the type of capital that they need to innovate new products, which creates new jobs.

The evidence on job creation is both surprising and somewhat scary. There appears to be a very small subset of firms, primarily related to technology innovation, that both directly create jobs inside of those companies, and spin off the greatest number of indirect employment multipliers in a very defined geographical area.

Of all small business jobs created, most are in existing small technology companies with operational revenues, not in entrepreneurial startup companies. And, the powder keg of job creation occurs in a very defined set of technology companies, generally called the nine high technology value clusters by Dr. Ed Feser, of the University of Illinois.

The nine high tech industrial value chains identified by Dr. Feser are: Chemicals, industrial machinery, aerospace equipment, motor vehicles and transportation equipment, household appliances, electronic equipment, biotech and pharmaceuticals and communications and IT software.

The scary part of this evidence is that job growth is concentrated in such a small set of defined technology value chains. The number of companies in the entire national universe of companies in America, upon which job creation depends, is in just a small sliver of all companies, and most of that job growth depends on technology commercialization and product innovation.

The base, or foundation of job creation, is both on a very small subset of companies, and the jobs created in any single company are very small. Thus, to overcome the destruction of about 15 million jobs in the American economy in the past several years, an enormous rate of job creation is required in hundreds of thousands of small technology firms.

And the product innovation in those small companies depends on the company obtaining growth capital. A second scary part of the picture is that from the moment the investment occurs, if the company is lucky enough to find growth capital, it takes about three years for new jobs to be created directly in the companies, and about another two years before the spin-off, or indirect jobs, are created in related companies in the industrial value chains.

Even if the company can obtain capital, there is nothing automatic or certain that an investment today in a small technology company will create jobs five years out in the future from the date of the capital investment.

Unlike the entrepreneurial startup companies, which garner most of the public relations and media attention, the small operational companies are generally not candidates for venture capital or angel investments because most firms are family-held or closely-held businesses that are not likely to be sold to outside investors, as would be the case for an entrepreneurial startup company.

In these small closely-held companies with operational cash flow, there is no definite path of exit allowing the outside equity investors to reap a quick capital gain through a stock sale or merger/acquisition. Investor profits from investment in most small operational companies is usually in the form of dividends or some form of revenue sharing, not a capital gain.

The capital required in an operational company to support product innovation is in very small units, usually less than $3 million, and often less than $750,000. The current capital marketplace is not well organized to meet the needs of small operational companies.

For example, the capital needed for new product innovation in operational companies aims at a potentially risky technology product commercialization, and most FDIC commercial banks are not really interested in providing funding, in any form, to support risky product innovation.

The repayment of a commercial bank loan would depend on a very uncertain stream of future revenues from a technology product that was unproven in the market.

Finally, the innovation for most small companies occurs in distinct metro regions, as a result of knowledge sharing that occurs in the inter-firm buying and selling in the local industrial value chains, also called regional supply chains. Like politics, most innovation is local and much of it is in small technology companies trying to get a new product out the front door.

Being mostly a local market phenomena, the investment in small company innovation requires local sources of capital who are willing to take a risk on the owners of the company. These problems for small companies in raising capital have been around for at least 100 years.

There is nothing really new about the capital market problems of small size, risky investments, limited sources of capital or the geographic locus of technology innovation for small technology companies.

With the re-imaging of the internet as a marketplace, most of these age-old problems can be solved. Some of the economic research on the geography of capital markets suggests that most companies raise capital within 50 miles of where they are located.

Most of the venture capital firms in Silicon Valley state on their website that they like to make investments in local companies because they like to be able to drive to the company in one day to check on the financial health of the company.

The idea of driving to a company in one day also explains two other important components of a local capital marketplace.

The second component concerns the geographical scope of technology innovation, which also occurs within this 50-mile envelope. Innovation is primarily a mental exercise in imagination and collaboration among very well-educated and highly skilled people, some of whom work in the local industrial value chains, often at the larger global corporations.

These knowledge-bearers meet each other in bars, and the golf course, and in business social networking events, and swap stories and knowledge about what problems they are trying to solve. The ideas that they come up with for solving problems are potential new products that could be commercialized.

For ideas involving brand new products, in brand new entrepreneurial startup companies, the local angel/venture capital market seems to work well. Generally, these local sources of capital like to hear about the new ideas as soon as they are hatched.

Most of the communication between knowledge-bearers and venture capitalists also takes place in bars and on the golf course, usually located with 50 miles of where the knowledge-bearers work and commute every day. For existing companies with a new product idea, however, the local angel/VC market does not work very well.

The owners and senior executives of operational companies still go to social networking events and the owners still like to describe to other people the ideas they have for the new product.

But, the most likely sources of capital that potentially could be interested in funding the idea generally do not hang out in these networking venues because their deal sourcing is through more formal business application procedures.

Finally, the 50-mile envelope affects the most hidden and misunderstood component of the local capital marketplace that contributes to deals getting funded. Funding an uncertain technology innovation takes a large amount of faith and trust that an investment made today will pay out profits in the future.

The investor must trust the company to be remunerated in the future, and the company must trust the investor to fulfill the capital commitment to make an investment.

Legal and moral philosophers sometimes call this envelope of trust the "Rule-of-Law." Because "trust," as a moral value, is exchanged in face-to-face communications, the envelope of trust also extends about 50 miles.

The moral value of trust in a capital market exchange requires face-to-face communication over an extended period of time allowing both parties to build up confidence and trust to do the deal both before and after the investment is made.

One of the main reasons so many new entrepreneurial ideas do not get funded by the venture capital model, usually less than 2 out of 10 ideas, involves this lack of trust. And, after the funding, the main reason the failure rate of entrepreneurial companies is so high, generally over 70% in the first three years, also involves the absence of trust and faith in the risky investment.

In the case of re-envisioning the internet as a local capital marketplace, the internet as a global communication technology would be supplemented by face-to-face meeting events in order to overcome many of the issues related to the 50-mile envelope of capital, innovation and trust.

One example of how this new idea may work can be seen by comparing the new model with the current angel/venture capital model for startup companies, where pre-screened and cherry-picked companies meet with a limited set of capital market sources.

The new web-based social networking would be complemented by monthly capital market events that served the same purpose as the current angel events. However, the new events would feature operational companies who needed capital to support innovation, and the audience would be all sources of capital and all third party professional service providers who lived and worked within 50 miles of the event.

One big difference between the old closed angel model and the new model is somewhat like the difference between proprietary software and the newer forms of open source software. In the case of local capital marketplaces, open source events facilitate capital, innovation and trust within a 50-mile envelope.

The open invitation events aims at attracting angels, venture capitalists, commercial bankers, asset based lenders, SBA lenders, SBIC firms, debt investors, and FINRA broker/dealers.

Another big, but very subtle difference, is the financial interests being served by the new model. In the new model, the focus of attention is on the financial interests of the private companies who need capital, and many of the attendees in the audience share both a financial and civic interest in helping the companies find funding because of the local economic development benefits associated with job creation.

In the older angel/venture capital model, most events are very heavily oriented to serving the exclusive financial interests of the investors, not the company that needs capital. In most of those cases, the standard operating procedure is for the investors to set the terms and conditions of the investment that are most favorable to the investors.

In the newer more open internet model, the great diversity of funding sources at the events leads to both open market competition to get a deal funded, and also leads to more collaboration among the sources of capital to put together both equity and debt deals in combinations of funding that are not generally available in the more exclusive angel and VC events.

The newer internet technology allows local events to be more easily promoted among a community of interested professionals who are members of networking groups in a specific metro region, like a LinkedIn capital market group or a MeetUp professional networking group.

The newer web-based administrative portals allows the company to better manage a capital raise by being able to communicate with multiple sources of capital simultaneously. This newer form of communication by the company tends to put the company in a stronger negotiating position with the different sources of capital that may be competing for the business of providing funding.

The main idea of the new online business model is to combine business networking, business customer relationship management, online blogging and event management under the hood of one metro regional website, self-styled as "The Metro Regional Capital Marketplace."

In the metro capital marketplace model, the company that is raising capital has its own company website, which acts as the main landing pad for many other internet websites and networking groups. Once outside users land on the company website, new web technology allows the company to manage communications with outside users with private pass-word protected portals.

The company website is connected to a much larger metro capital marketplace website, where the three parties in the city can meet each other and schedule events for making presentations. The company can use the webinar software on the metro capital marketplace to manage national webinar presentations, using the customer relations module to screen and qualify viewers before access is granted to the webinar.

The main idea behind the new business model is that each party to a capital market exchange can use the new framework to make money and participate in deals, almost as soon as they are hatched.

The company is in a much stronger position to negotiate the terms and conditions, and to combine the different forms of capital required, in the small units needed by the company to fund product innovation. When the internet is re-imagined in a new way, as a local interactive capital marketplace, it can provide new channels of communication between the three parties to a capital market exchange.

Investors can use the new networks to discover ideas and possible deals, the companies that need capital can use the internet to allow investors to investigate their company, and the wide variety of third party professional advisors, who act as intermediaries between buyers and sellers of capital can find new clients in the social networks.

Much of the technology for allowing the internet to function in this new model already exist, but the different linkages between websites, and the new software coding on a single website, have not been organized into a business model where all the parties to the exchange can use the internet functionality to make money.

Part of the re-imagining of the internet involves a slight change in the end goals to which the new model is directed. In the current conception of using the internet to help companies raise capital, the main focus has been on serving the financial needs of the sources of capital, such as the venture capital firms.

In the new business model, the end goal is to serve the capital market needs of small companies who use the internet to raise capital to fund product innovation.

And the great social benefit derived from this slight change in philosophy is that by increasing competition and doing more private capital market deals, a much greater rate of job creation in a metro regional economy can be achieved.

Targeting capital investments into a regional technology value chain increases the regional income and employment multipliers, which further stimulates cumulative on-going innovation.

Those future rounds of innovation will need for more capital, and if the local capital markets continue to work well, then profits from the earlier investments can easily be reinvested back into the local economy. That process is called self-renewing free market economic growth.

Much of the current legal status of CrowdFunding is shrouded in myths and misperceptions about the entire capital market, and the disproportionate attention given to the role of venture capital, compared to all Reg D funding.

The myths are a big reason why the SEC was so slow about implementing the rules for both Title II and Title III CrowdFunding, under the JOBS Act of 2012. For Accredited Investor (Title II) the SEC missed the Congressional goal of implementation of rules by about 18 months.

This books begins by explaining what the five big myths are related to CrowdFunding.

Myth #1: Private capital market transactions that promote economic development rely on VCs and angels as the primary sources of capital.
The total Reg D Rule 506 private placement market in 2012 provided about $800 billion in capital to deals, and the 144A market added about $700 billion.

For comparison, the best guess of all venture capital in 2012 invested in private deals was about $26.5 billion in 3,698 deals. (MoneyTree Report by PricewaterhouseCoopers LLP and the National Venture Capital Association, based on data from Thomson Reuters).

In the more recent years, the entire investments of venture capital firms was about $30 billion.

In other words, the entire amount of VC/angel capital invested in 2012 deals was about 1.5% of the total capital invested in private deals, allowing for some minor statistical data issues of double counting from both sources of data.

The important point about this data for promoting technology based economic development, as it relates to Myth #1, is that Rule 144A capital is nearly as big, and as important, as all Reg D capital.

Economic development professionals would want to expand their framework of how Reg D capital fits into a larger capital market by including 144A offerings. In the logical chronology of events surrounding technology based economic development, Reg D offerings occur first, and then later, as if capital funding occurred in a pipeline of deals, 144A offerings occur to assist the early investors take their gains and exit the deal.

The venture capital and angel funding is significant at the very earliest stages of the deal pipeline, but it is a very small part of the bigger capital market picture.

Myth #2: There is rampant fraud in private securities offerings.

Section 501 of the 2002 Uniform Securities Act, titled "General Fraud," states that it is unlawful, in connection with the offer, sale, or purchase of a security, to employ a device, scheme, or artifice to defraud; to make an untrue statement of material fact; to omit to state a material fact; or to engage in an act, practice, or course of business that operates as a fraud or deceit upon another person.

The North American Securities Administrators Association (NASAA) is comprised of
U. S. state securities officials, who coordinate regulation of state investment advisors and stock brokers, across state lines.

Each year, NASAA prepares a report on the cases of fraud that its members investigate. The survey traditionally gauges the extent and prevalence of enforcement efforts by state securities regulators, and identifies trends and issues in national investor protection.

The 2012 NASAA enforcement report states, "The majority of fraud cases featured unregistered individuals selling unregistered securities. More than 800 reported actions involved unregistered securities, and more than 800 actions involved unregistered firms or individuals." (2012 Enforcement Report, Prepared by NASAA Enforcement Section, Washington, D. C., October 2012)

"A total of 632 reported actions involved unregistered individuals and 485 actions involved unregistered firms," the report continues. "This compares to 399 reported actions against investment adviser firms, the largest number of actions in any registered category and nearly double the reported investment adviser actions the year before. There were 359 reported actions against registered broker dealers and 297 actions against registered broker dealer agents. In addition, 151 actions were taken against investment adviser representatives."

To place this data in its accurate context, NASAA members regulate about 20,000 state registered investment advisors, and in 2012, there were about 18,000 new Reg D Form D filings for private offerings. As stated by the SEC report on public solicitation rules, "For the year ended December 31, 2012, 16,067 issuers made 18,187 new Form D filings, of which 15,208 issuers relied on the Rule 506 exemption. Based on the information reported by issuers on Form D, there were 3,958 small issuers."

In other words, out of 20,000 state registered investment advisors, and over 18,000 Reg D private securities offerings, involving 4000 companies, NASAA captured 151 advisor representatives and captured about 800 firms who were not properly registered in 2012.

The SEC also emphasized the issue of fraud in Reg D offerings in its July 10, 2013, report on rules for securities public solicitation. The SEC report cited an independent scholarly economic research article on actions involved with rights of rescission of contracts, when a Reg D offering goes bad. (Eliminating the Prohibition on General Solicitation and General Advertising in Certain Offerings, FACT SHEET, SEC Open Meeting, July 10, 2013).

In this case, investors in a bad deal have the right to rescind their contract, and get their investment money back from the company.

As the SEC reports notes, "A more recent study has identified 245 lawsuits (both federal and state) involving 200 venture capitalists as defendants between 1975 and 2007, and has shown that VC funds that are older and have a larger presence in terms of size and network are less likely to be sued." (Vladimir Atanasov, Vladimir Ivanov, and Kate Litvak, Does Reputation Limit Opportunistic Behavior in the VC Industry? Evidence From Litigation Against VCs, 67 Journal of Finance 2215 (2012)

To summarize the research report on fraud, cited by the SEC, over a 22 year period of time, in both state and federal courts, the SEC report notes a total of 245 lawsuits involving venture capital firms related to Reg D offerings, some of which may have involved fraud.

The important point about busting Myth #2 for understanding CrowdFunding is that it is important to be able to recognize fraud when you see it, but that the issue of fraud is primarily a political red-herring that is being dragged across the floor by opponents of CrowdFunding to delay and limit its implementation.

Myth #3: Most Reg D private offerings involve new venture, entrepreneurial startups.

Most Reg D offerings in the past four years have been for established, operational companies, with top line revenues in a range of around $1 million, according to the SEC report on rules for public solicitation. The median size of the Reg D offering was $1.5 million in 2012.

The July 10, 2013, SEC report continues, "Offerings conducted in reliance on Rule 506 account for 99% of the capital reported as being raised under Regulation D from 2009 to 2012, and represent approximately 94% of the number of Regulation D offerings. The significance of Rule 506 offerings is underscored by the comparison to registered offerings.

In 2012, the estimated amount of capital reported as being raised in Rule 506 offerings (including both equity and debt) was $898 billion, compared to $1.2 trillion raised in registered offerings. Of this $898 billion, operating companies (issuers that are not pooled investment funds) reported raising $173 billion, while pooled investment funds reported raising $725 billion."

As the SEC report states, "An analysis of all Form D filings submitted between 2009 to 2012 shows that approximately 11% of all new Regulation D offerings reported sales commissions of greater than zero because the issuers used a broker intermediary.

The average commission paid to these intermediaries was 5.9% of the offering size, with the median commission being approximately 5%. Accordingly, for a $5 million offering, which was the median size of a Regulation D offering with a commission during this period, an issuer could potentially save up to $250,000 if it solicits investors directly rather than through an intermediary..."

In other words, over a 4-year period, only 11 percent of the Reg D offerings involved the payment of commissions, yet this 11% of the market is driving the political red-herring agenda at the SEC in issuing rules on CrowdFunding.

For the median offering of $5 million that involve commissions for the venture capital intermediary, those small firms will save an average of $250,000 in commissions by conducting a Reg D Rule 506c CrowdFunding self-underwriting.

Myth #4: There are not many investors who will be interested in CrowdFunding, and therefore the status quo approach under Title II of the JOBS Act is the most important focus.

The NASAA report cited above suggests that there are only a small number of potential accredited investors who may be interested in CrowdFunding. This statement about the future numbers of potential accredited investors for CrowdFunding is a myth.

There are about 8 million individual investors, in about 5 million U. S. households, with incomes that would qualify as a potential Reg D accredited investor under the Reg D Rule 506c rules for CrowdFunding. More importantly for regional economic development strategy, clusters of very wealthy investors exist in distinct geographical locations, primarily in the 350 U. S. metro regions with over 150,000 population.

That population of potential accredited investors in each metro region has an existing affinity interest in promoting local economic development in their home communities.

According to the data in the SEC report on solicitation, about 234,000 accredited investors made Reg D investments in 2012. As the SEC report states, "In 2012, approximately 153,000 investors participated in offerings by operating companies, while approximately 81,000 investors invested in offerings by pooled investment funds."

The 153,000 investors who made direct investments in operating companies are the target market for economic developers who want to integrate CrowdFunding into regional economic strategy. They were primarily individual investors, not angels or venture capitalists, who made investments in existing operational companies, not entrepreneurial new ventures.

The 81,000 investors who made Reg D investments in pooled funds, primarily invested in venture capital limited partnerships, and the VCs then turned around and invested in private deals, primarily the type of deals that look a lot like the ones that come from the university tech transfer office.

In busting Myth # 4, the language used to describe potential Reg D Rule 506 investors would make a clear distinction between the 153,000 investors who made direct investments, and the 81,000 investors who made investments through pooled accounts.
The 153,000 direct investors are generally called "Lone Wolf Investors."
The 81,000 other investors are commonly called "Angels."

Myth #5: The financial interests and legal rights of non-accredited investors should be the primary public policy focus on implementing CrowdFunding rules.

In its September 2012 proposed rules on eliminating the prohibition on general public solicitation of a Reg D offering, the SEC combined a long and complicated list of factors that a company must first assess, before they could raise CrowdFunding capital. (Federal Register/Vol. 77, No. 172/Wednesday, September 5, 2012 /Proposed Rules).

The SEC proposed rules stated, "These factors are interconnected, and the information gained by looking at these factors would help an issuer assess the reasonable likelihood that a potential purchaser is an accredited investor, which would, in turn, affect the types of steps that would be reasonable to take to verify a purchaser's accredited investor status.

Seven months later, as the SEC July 10, 2013 final rules noted, "90 percent of the Regulation D offerings conducted between 2009 and 2012 did not involve any non-accredited investors."

In other words, the political red herring of fraud in Reg D offerings is connected to the exploitation of non-accredited investors, but the evidence suggests that non-accredited investors are not a significant population of Reg D investors.

More than two thirds of all Reg D private offerings in 2012 had 10 or fewer investors, and less than 5% of all offerings had more than 30 investors.

In other words, 95 percent of Reg D offerings in 2012 involved less than 30 investors per deal and involved very small amounts of capital, invested in very small operational companies, with very few non-accredited investors.

Most of the small Reg D deals between 2009 and 2012 involved equity, and almost 1/3 of all offerings during that period involved the issuance of bonds, not stock or equity interests.

As the SEC noted, "Between 2009 and 2012, approximately 66% of Regulation D offerings were of equity securities, and almost two-thirds of these were by issuers other than pooled investment funds."

In busting Myth #5, it is important to remember that The JOBS Act was not passed by Congress in order to help the CEO of a small company assess the credentials of an investor. The main public policy goal addressed by the JOBS Act is how to stimulate economic growth and job creation by small technology companies.

The SEC's accredited investor CrowdFunding rules on general solicitation continue a confusing commingling by the SEC staff that misapplies rules assoc 1934 Securities Exchange Act, related to brokers as intermediaries, to the 1958 Rules on Reg D 506 offerings.

Part of understanding the current political and legal status of accredited investor CrowdFunding is to understand that the internet has outpaced the ability of the SEC to apply logical rules to the use of the internet to raise capital.

The new SEC regulations of raising capital under Reg D 506c are based on the traditional venture capital model that a private company goes to a venture capital firm or angel partnership and seeks capital. The internet has made that earlier model obsolete, but the current SEC CrowdFunding rules continue to misapply the earlier rules to accredited investor CrowdFunding.

Part of the effect of this misapplication of the rules will make it more difficult for companies to raise capital and therefore tend to undermine the intent of Congress in passing the JOBS Act aimed at making a capital raise easier, not harder.

The historical origins of the misapplication is partially related to the SEC Angel Capital Network no action letter, which s Re: Angel Capital Electronic Network a "broker" is defined in Section 3(a)(4) of the Exchange Act as a person engaged "in the business of effecting transactio and a "dealer" is defined in Section 3(a)(5) of the Exchange Act as a person engaged "in the business of buying and selling securities.

The Division's interpretive letter IPONet was based on an important and well-known principle established by the 1934 Ac passage of the 1958 Reg D rules: a general solicitation is not present when there is a pre-existing, substantive relationship issuer, or its broker-dealer, and the offerees.

The language for "knowing your customer" is taken from the 1934 Act regarding a broker's obligations and is then applie placements as they may occur in the 1958 Reg D rules for a private placement.

In other words, beginning with the IPONet letter, the SEC commingled the 1934 language of a broker "knowing his client rules, which are related to the 1933 Securities Act. The more burdensome rules contained in the IPONet letter are now being applied to internet crowd funding private placements.

In the IPONET no-action letter, IPONET's activities will not amount to general solicitation or general advertising as long as:
both the invitation to complete the questionnaire and the questionnaire itself must be generic in nature and may not offering;

the password-protected page containing offerings may become available to a particular investor only after the IPO that the particular investor is accredited or sophisticated; and
the potential investor may purchase securities only after the point in time at which that investor has qualified as an accredited or sophisticated investor.

This same logic was applied by the SEC in Shaine (1987). A preexisting substantive relationship for purposes of general s under Rule 502(c) may be established through the proper use of a satisfactory questionnaire (as submitted). See letter re Co., Inc. dated March 31, 1987.

Shaine determined accredited status by having potential investors complete questionnaires designed to evaluate each potential investor's sophistication and financial resources.

In the IPOnet No-Action Letter, the SEC stated that "the qualifications of accredited investors manner described and the posting of a notice concerning a private fund on a Web site that is password-protected and accessed by subscribers who are pre-determined to be Accredited Investors would not involve a "general solicitation" or 'general advertising' within the meaning of rule 502(c) of Securities Act Regulation D."

To summarize, the internet has opened up new pathways to raise capital, and the new websites are one response on how to use the internet to make money helping companies raise capital. The SEC rules on CrowdFunding do not accommodate either development, and therefore tend to retard capital formation for small companies.

Chapter 4. The Location of Accredited Investor CrowdFunding in the Universe of Private Capital Markets

The big picture of private capital markets can best be visualized as three parties to a private capital market transaction. The three parties to the transaction are:
- The demand side of the market, meaning all firms and entities, including nascent entrepreneurs, who need capital, in any form.
- The supply side of the market, meaning any source of capital or funding.
- The professional intermediaries who provide services to either firms or sources of capital, so that a transaction can take place.

Diagram 3. Visualizing the Entire Private Capital Market As A Transaction

The Demand for Capital	Professional Intermediaries Who Service The Transactions	The Supply of Capital

The word "private" has a dual interpretation. The companies who need capital are private, in the sense that their securities do not trade in a public marketplace. Public stock markets are regulated under the 1934 Securities Market Act.

Another common term for private, that CPAs use, to describe private firms is "closely-held," meaning that the ownership is held by a very small group of people. For example, in the case of a small family business, the two owners may be the husband and wife, which would describe a closely-held family company.

Private also means that the securities issued by a company are not registered under the 1933 Securities Act, and are restricted in how and where the securities can be sold.

Accredited Investor CrowdFunding is located under the demand side of the market, because a company is issuing either stocks or bonds that are not registered with the U. S. Securities and Exchange Commission, and the securities, after being issued to new investors, are not going to trade, or be exchanged, in a public stock exchange, like the National Association of Securities Dealers Automated Quote System (NASDAQ).

Diagram 4. The Demand Side of the Market

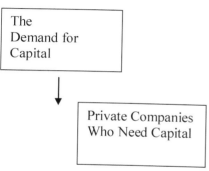

The
Demand for
Capital

Private Companies
Who Need Capital

Accredited investors could be anyone, or any type of organization, that meets one of the 8 classifications and criteria that are contained under a provision of the securities rules called Regulation D, Rule 501. While most of the media attention for CrowdFunding has focused on natural biological persons, who either earn over $200,000, or have over $1 million in net worth, the definition of accredited investors is much broader.

Diagram 5. Section 501 Accredited Investors Are Part of the Supply Side of the Rule 506c

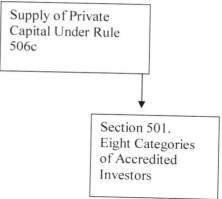

Supply of Private
Capital Under Rule
506c

Section 501.
Eight Categories
of Accredited
Investors

A company conducting an accredited investor CrowdFunding may sell its private securities to any of the 8 categories that are defined in Section 501 as "accredited investors."

The federal securities laws define the 8 categories of the term accredited investor in Rule 501 of Regulation D as:

- a bank, insurance company, registered investment company, business development company, or small business investment company;

- an employee benefit plan, within the meaning of the Employee Retirement Income Security Act, if a bank, insurance company, or registered investment adviser makes the investment decisions, or if the plan has total assets in excess of $5 million;
- a charitable organization, corporation, or partnership with assets exceeding $5 million;
- a director, executive officer, or general partner of the company selling the securities;
- a business in which all the equity owners are accredited investors;
- a natural person who has individual net worth, or joint net worth with the person's spouse, that exceeds $1 million at the time of the purchase, excluding the value of the primary residence of such person;
- a natural person with income exceeding $200,000 in each of the two most recent years or joint income with a spouse exceeding $300,000 for those years and a reasonable expectation of the same income level in the current year; or
- a trust with assets in excess of $5 million, not formed to acquire the securities offered, whose purchases a sophisticated person makes.

Diagram 6. Classification of The Components of the Supply Side of the Private Capital Markets

Type of Capital or Title	Function and Regulatory Oversight
Accredited Investors	Defined under Section 501 of the 1982 Amendments to the 1933 Securities Act.
Non-accredited Investors	Originally defined in certain sections of the 1982 Reg D rules, and more recently defined in Title III of the 2012 JOBS Act.
Angel Partnerships and Venture Capital Funds	Firms that aggregate investment capital from multiple sources, usually with professional advisors and manager. Defined in the 1934 Securities Market Act, the 1940 Investment Company Act, and more recently, in the Dodd Frank Act.
Closed End Mutual Funds	Professional mutual funds whose shares trade in a public market. Some funds specifically target investments to private companies. So, while any investor can buy shares of the fund, a mutual fund with an investment goal of investing in private company fund turns around and buys shares of private companies, just like a venture capital firm. The Closed End Fund is regulated by the 1940 Investment Company Act, the 1940 Investment Advisors Act, and more recently, under certain provisions of the Dodd Frank Act.
FINRA Broker Dealers	Professional firms comprised of brokers who make a market between buyers and sellers of capital. Both the firm itself, and all the brokers, are registered agents, and regulated by a giant regulatory agency called FINRA. FINRA is authorized to regulate under certain provisions of the 1934 Securities Market Act. Brokers who are registered agents, under the 1934 Securities Market Act, can hold dual registration as a registered investment advisor, under the 1940 Investment Advisor Act. All brokers and all investment advisors are bound by the anti-fraud provisions of multiple agencies and laws.
Private Equity Hedge Funds	Professional mutual funds, which until very recently, were not required to register as a mutual fund, under the provisions of the 1940 Investment Company Act. The term "hedge" implies that the managers of the fund would invest in many types of investments, including private companies, in order to hedge the risk to investors. Most recently, the Dodd Frank Act requires many hedge funds to register as a mutual fund, under the provisions of the 1940 Investment Company Act.
Investment Banking Firms	Investment banking firms provide professional services in merger and acquisitions, primarily between very large companies, that want to buy smaller companies, or between many smaller firms that would perform better if they were managed by a single management structure. In the late 1980's, the investment banking firms also engaged in breaking up bigger companies into much smaller companies. In most cases, the investment banks avoid registration under the 1940 Investment Advisor Act, but sometimes, they perform activities related to Rule 144A transactions, and are regulated under the 1982 amendments to the 1933 Securities Act.
FDIC Commercial Banks	FDIC banks are known as depository banks, and are regulated by the Federal Deposit Insurance Corporation, an agency authorized by the U. S. Congress to regulate the banks. The FDIC is a component of a much bigger financial and monetary regulatory structure called the Federal Reserve Bank, whose regional divisions are called the Federal Reserve System. Most commercial banks have a division that makes loans to small businesses, and also provides commercial credit cards to private companies. Until 1998, most FDIC banks could not also function as broker dealers, under the provisions of FINRA. More recently, FDIC banks can be registered as both an FDIC bank and a FINRA broker dealer. FDIC bank can be registered agents of the Small Business Administration, and be authorized to make SBA guaranteed loans to a small private company.
Commercial Finance Asset Based Lenders and Factors	Asset based lenders function like FDIC banks in the sense that they make capital and loans available to private companies. The loans are secured and collateralized by the private company's assets. If the private company fails to pay its loan, the asset based lender has the right to sell the assets of the company. In most cases, the asset based lenders are not registered agents with either FINRA, FDIC, or the 1940 Investment Company Act.
Small Business Investment Companies (SBICs)	An SBIC is authorized to provide financial services to small private companies, under the provisions of different Federal laws, including the 1940 Investment Company Act, the Small Business Administration Act, and the 1940 Investment Advisors Act.

A common misperception in the media is that venture capital firms are classified as "accredited investors," under the Regulation D Rule 501 definitions. The rules governing venture capital firms and angel partnerships are not contained in Reg D, but are located in other parts of the U. S. securities laws.

The SEC definitions of a VC fund are contained in several different laws, the two most important of which are the Dodd–Frank Wall Street Reform and Consumer Protection Act, and the 1940 Investment Company Act.

In order to avoid registering as a mutual fund, under the 1940 Investment Company Act, a VC fund must:

- be a "private fund" – i.e., an entity that would be an investment company under the Investment Company Act of 1940 (the "Investment Company Act"), but for the exceptions provided under sections 3(c)(1) or 3(c)(7) of that act.
- hold itself out in the media and public relations as a VC Fund. A VC Fund must represent to investors that it pursues a venture capital strategy.
- must invest in and hold "qualifying investments" in "qualifying portfolio companies" ("QPCs") and short-term investments. A QPC is generally a company that (1) is not an SEC-reporting company or publicly traded, (2) does not borrow and distribute the proceeds of the borrowing to the VC Fund in connection with its investment in the QPC, and (3) is not itself a fund (i.e., it must be an operating company).

Generally, a company undertaking an accredited investor CrowdFunding project would not target venture capital firms as a source of capital, and most venture capital firms would not be interested in funding most CrowdFunding projects.

A venture capital firm pools capital together from many different types of investors, some of whom may also be accredited investors. The venture capital fund looks like, and functions like, a mutual fund, generally with an advisor who makes investment recommendations to a Board, who votes to make an investment in a company.

The venture capital firm raises its funds by asking potential investors to promise to provide future funds when the fund gets company prospects lined up for investment. The potential investors could be other venture capital firms, bankers, or individual accredited investors.

At the time that the venture capital firm needs the capital, it makes a telephone call, known as the "capital call," to the investors who promised to make the investment. When the investor receives the call, they transfer the funds to the firm, which then makes the investment in the company.

In contrast to an accredited investor CrowdFunding project, the venture capital fund will usually set the terms and conditions for the securities that the venture capital firm intends to buy from the company, while under accredited investor CrowdFunding, the company sets the terms and conditions.

In CrowdFunding, if the accredited investor likes the deal, they may invest. They had not previously promised to make an investment, so in accredited investor CrowdFunding, there is no capital call. The accredited investor conducts self-guided due diligence and makes a decision to invest or not invest.

The great majority of all private placements in the U. S. take place under an exemption from registration as a public offering under a set of rules adopted by the U. S. Securities and Exchange Commission in 1982 called Regulation D.

Parts of Reg D were modified by a law in 1996 that exempted certain private securities from state regulatory oversight. Rule 506 offerings are not subject to review in the 50 states. As a result of the modifications to Reg D Rule 506, about 90% of all private capital is raised under the provisions of Rule 506, which is the same rule that was modified by the 2012 JOBS Act.

In the two years between September 15, 2008 and October 18, 2010, for example, there were a total of 27,234 Reg D offerings, of which 25,591 (94%) were issued under Rule 506.

For a more recent comparison, for the entire year ended December 31, 2012, there were a total of 18,187 Reg D filings, of which 15,208 (84%) relied on the Rule 506 exemption.

Section 501, of Reg D, cited above for its rules defining accredited investors, was added in 1982, at the same time as Section 506. According to data released by the SEC, about $800 billion of private placements occurred in 2012, issued under the provisions of Reg D.

The chart below was, prepared by the SEC, shows the total amount of private capital issued in the U. S. between 2009 and 2012, shows how private securities issued under all Regulation D compared with both the securities issued in public markets.

Diagram 7. Capital Raised in U.S. Capital Markets During 2009-2012

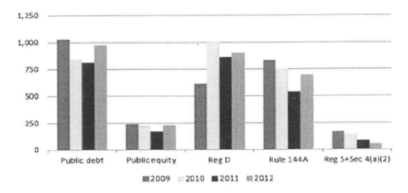

Figure 1: Capital Raised in U.S. Capital Markets during 2009-2012[197]

Data Taken From Diagram 1 of the Statement at the SEC Open Meeting by Chairwoman Mary Jo White, U.S. Securities and Exchange Commission, Eliminating the Prohibition on General Solicitation and General Advertising in Certain Offerings, July 10, 2013, Washington DC

The Reg D private placement market in 2012 provided about $800 billion in capital to deals, and the 144A market added an additional $700 billion. The 144A security transactions represent secondary sales of private securities, after the mandated holding period of the initial private placements.

In the logical chronology of events surrounding accredited investor CrowdFunding, Reg D offerings occur first, and then later, 144A offerings occur to assist the early investors to take their gains and exit the deal.

In other words, 144A transactions are made by a very select group of investors, known as Qualified Institutional Buyers, (QIBs), who buy private securities from the first round of investors, many of whom were accredited investors, as defined by Rule 501.

In many cases, the lapse of time between the initial issuance of securities and the subsequent sale, under Rule 144A, is very short, suggesting that a prior agreement had been reached between the firms in the Reg D part of the capital market and the Rule 144A part of the market.

This short period of time is one reason why the SEC data lumps Reg D transactions together with Rule 144A transactions, for a total private capital investment in 2012 of $1.5 trillion.

For a comparison between accredited investors and venture capitalist transactions, the best guess of all venture capital in 2012 invested in private deals was about $26.5 billion in 3,698 deals. (MoneyTree Report by PricewaterhouseCoopers LLP and the National Venture Capital Association, based on data from Thomson Reuters).

In other words, the entire amount of VC/angel capital invested in 2012 deals was about 1.5% of the total capital of $800 billion invested in Reg D private deals, allowing for some minor statistical data issues of double counting from both sources of data.

The venture capital and angel funding is significant at the top of the deal pipeline, targeted to the very earliest stages of a company, but it is a very small part of the bigger capital market picture.

The universe of potential accredited investors, who are natural persons, and not banks or other legal entities in the supply side of the market, is vastly bigger than the universe of venture capital firms. There are about 1000 venture capital firms, with an average of 8 employees. About 40% of all venture capital investments occur in one state, California.

In comparison, there are about 5 million U. S. households with incomes that would qualify as a potential Reg D accredited investor under the Reg D Rule 506c rules for CrowdFunding. The data on households translates roughly into about 8 million citizens, who could potentially make an accredited investor CrowdFunding investment.

Only a tiny fraction of the 8 million potential investors actually made investments in 2012. According to the data in the SEC report on solicitation, about 234,000 accredited investors made Reg D investments in 2012.

As the SEC report states, "In 2012, approximately 153,000 investors participated in offerings by operating companies, while approximately 81,000 investors invested in offerings by pooled investment funds."

The 153,000 investors who made direct investments in operating companies represent the prototype target market for most CEOs who are using accredited investor CrowdFunding to raise capital.

In other words, those 153,000 investors serve as the prototype for soliciting investors. They were primarily individual investors, not angels or venture capitalists, and the accredited investors made investments primarily in existing operational companies, not entrepreneurial new ventures.

The 81,000 investors who made Reg D investments in pooled funds, primarily invested in venture capital limited partnerships, and the VC firms then turned around and invested in private deals.

The VC firms had lined up the 81,000 investors with the earlier promises, or letters of commitment, that the investors signed, when they promised to make future investments.

The 153,000 accredited investors who made independent decisions are generally called "Lone Wolf Investors." The 81,000 other individual accredited investors, who invested through the venture capital firms are commonly called "Angels."

Sometimes, the angels band together and form their own legal entities, called angel partnerships, which look and act just like venture capital firms. The angel partnerships usually have a professional investment advisor, or manager, who screens investment deals, and makes recommendations to the Board of Directors of the angel partnership.

For comparison, most Reg D investments in 2012, were made by individual accredited investors. The SEC report of July 10, 2013 final rules noted, "90 percent of the Regulation D offerings conducted between 2009 and 2012 did not involve any non-accredited investors."

More than two thirds of all Reg D private offerings in 2012 had 10 or fewer investors, and less than 5% of all offerings had more than 30 investors. In other words, 95 percent of Reg D offerings in 2012 involved less than 30 investors per deal and involved very small amounts of capital, invested in very small operational companies, with very few non-accredited investors.

Most of the small Reg D deals between 2009 and 2012 involved equity, and almost 1/3 of all offerings during that period involved the issuance of bonds, not stock or equity interests. As the SEC noted, "Between 2009 and 2012, approximately 66% of Regulation D offerings were of equity securities, and almost two-thirds of these were by issuers other than pooled investment funds."

While the activity of Reg D accredited investors is significant in the world of private capital markets, the segment is only one small component of a much bigger universe of supply of capital. The supply side of the market could be classified by type of capital or service, as described in Diagram 5.

Accredited investors are free to invest capital in many different components of the private capital market, and can "pool," or aggregate capital with other investors, to obtain professional management of their investments.

For example, an accredited investor may decide to invest in a venture capital firm, and also in a hedge fund.

The big change for accredited investor CrowdFunding is that accredited investors have an easier path to directly invest in a small private company. Prior to the passage of the 2012 JOBS Act, a company that needed capital was prohibited from marketing and advertising to potential investors, and consequently, most potential investors never heard news about the funding opportunity.

This prohibition on advertising and marketing, that was amended by the 2012 JOBS Act, tended to create a monopoly for venture capital and angel capital firms, who had an advantage in learning about the investment opportunity. A monopoly on the supply side of the capital market is called a monopsony by economists, which means an unfair non-competitive advantage in the supply of a good or service.

Sometimes, in the older model, the private capital market monopsony set onerous terms and conditions for companies, who did not have other sources of capital available. The monopsony of private capital meant that many small companies could not raise growth capital unless they agreed to the onerous terms and conditions of the monopsonists.

Under the older monopsony model, the deck was stacked against the financial interests of companies, and the newer Reg D Rule 506(c) rules on advertising and marketing tend to reduce the advantages of the monopsonists, while at the same time, making the responsibilities of the professional advisors more important for protecting the financial interests of the private company that is issuing securities.

The supply and demand sides of the private capital market are brought together for transactions by a complex set of business professional intermediaries. Accredited investor CrowdFunding places a greater emphasis on this part of the capital market because private companies will be issuing securities directly to investors, with the help of their professional advisors.

This part of the private capital market is often overlooked because the conventional economic treatment of supply and demand curves usually only shows two lines that intersect at equilibrium. Hidden behind that easy-to-understand graph is a very complicated set of relationships that helps the participants to a market exchange find each other and execute a transaction.

While most of the media attention of the function of intermediaries between buyers and sellers of capital is on the securities attorneys who assist the company in preparing the offering documents, the range of professionals involved in facilitating a CrowdFunding offering is much bigger.

Diagram 8 describes this large range of possible business intermediaries that would become involved in an accredited investor CrowdFunding project.

Diagram 8. Business Professional Intermediaries Provide Services That Service Financial Transactions. Intermdediaries "Make" the Market

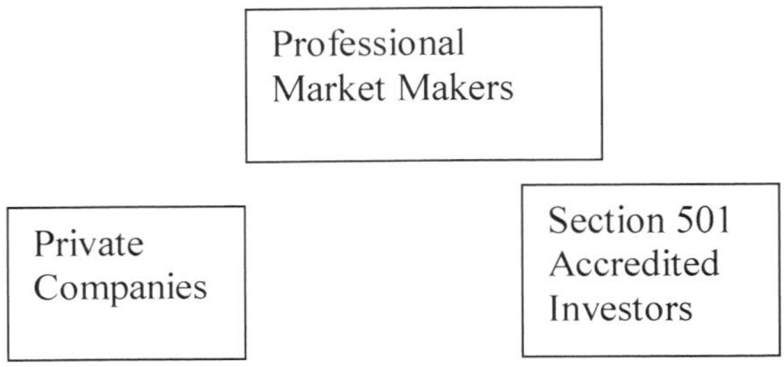

	Professional Market Makers

Private Companies	Section 501 Accredited Investors

Diagram 9 provides more detail about the firms who comprise the professional intermediaries.

Diagram 9. The Range of Business Professional Intermediaries Involved In An Accredited Investor CrowdFunding Project

Type of Business Intermediary	Function of Intermediary in Accredited Investor Crowdfund
Professional economic development associations and trade groups, like economic development partnerships and chambers of commerce	Promotes the financial interests of member firms and the economic growth prospects of regions. Coordinates resources within regions to facilitate technology innovation and capital market transactions.
Registered Investment Advisors	Acts as a fiduciary to the private company in providing advice, and conducts third party verification of the potential investor's credentials.
Marketing and sales professionals	Coordinates the marketing of the company's offering with other marketing and sales efforts of the company during the period of the CrowdFunding project.
Product design and prototype firms	Assists the company in product re-design for existing products or helps prototype new products.
Media and public relations firms	Prepares and distributes news stories and press releases for company and helps the company develop a market message.
Business life insurance agents	Assists the owners in creating a business buy-sell agreement
Business property and casualty agents	Assists the owners with issues involving product liability, owner liability and professional errors and omissions related to offering securities.
Employee benefit firms	Provides guidance and advice related to how additional capital may affect existing employee benefit arrangements, including non-qualified deferred compensation related to employee stock options on new capital.
Commercial real estate brokers and development firms	Provides real estate leasing guidance and brokerage for new facilities for firms. Assists firms within an industrial cluster to locate close to each other.
Business buy/sell brokers and investment bankers	Assists companies in finding new partners and new sources of supply.
CPAs and tax advisors to firms	Prepares statements related to an offering, including the statements for companies that fall into categories that require audited statements to raise capital.
Securities lawyers	Creates offering documents and legal agreements for a private offering. Provides advice and counsel to owners to meet rules. Answers questions about the offering for investor inquiries.
Professional Association Event Managers	Conducts business networking events for companies to present their message to interested parties to the transaction.
Trade Show Event Managers	Conducts events for companies within a trade group or trade association.
Capital Market and VC Event Managers	Conducts events for investors interested in learning more about a company.
Mobile Application Firms	Places company offering promotions on mobile devices.
Mobile Device Firms	Provides mobile devices for company.
Software and Coding Firms	Creates software that makes company promotional material available on mobile devices.
Website and eCommerce Developers	Assists the company in website development related to investor relations. Coordinates company website with outside websites to direct viewers to due diligence websites.
Social Network Marketing Firms	Assists the company in website optimization and social networking linkages on outside sites like LinkedIn.
Angel Matching Websites	Provides internet websites that aggregate potential investors who want to have a flow of information about companies that are raising capital

One big difference between the old monopsony venture capital model and the new accredited investor CrowdFunding model is the ability of the company to select the range and options to issue the securities by selecting the right set of advisors.

Under the older model, the initiative for selecting the professional business intermediaries usually remained with the monopsonists. Under the new model, the company can customize the set of investment advisors, and has a greater ability to control the costs associated with retaining the advisors.

To summarize, the big picture of private capital markets can best be visualized as three parties to a private capital market transaction. The three parties to the transaction are:

The demand side of the market, meaning all firms and entities, including nascent entrepreneurs, who need capital, in any form.

The supply side of the market, meaning any source of capital or funding.

The professional intermediaries who provide services to either firms or sources of capital, so that a transaction can take place.

Within that very big picture, a smaller part of the market is related to Reg D private offerings. Within Reg D, there is a brand new type of offering called Reg D Rule 506(c), commonly called "accredited investor CrowdFunding."

It is important to remember that the term "CrowdFunding" can be used to describe many different types of CrowdFunding, including charitable giving and non-accredited investor CrowdFunding.

There are no common or accepted usages of the term, either in professional journals or the mass media. This book is about Reg D Rule 506c, commonly called "Accredited Investor CrowdFunding.

Chapter 5. Overview of The Reg D Rule 506(c) CrowdFunding Websites

This chapter is about the 25 U. S. websites that are categorized by Crowdsourcing.org as those targeting investments to either operational, established companies that seek either accredited investors, under the rules for marketing private placements established by Title II of the JOBS Act of 2012.

A unique category of about 30 CrowdFunding websites is starting to emerge, as can be seen in the Diagram under "business lending" sites.

This is a new development in CrowdFunding that may have originated in Europe, where the activity is commonly called "peer-to-peer" lending. The capital activity resembles the type of loans made by commercial banks to a small company, except that in this new model, the company is making an appeal for loans to a much bigger crowd. This book does not address the business lending websites.

Many of the 25 newer internet CrowdFunding websites continue the logic and direction of causation of the earlier matching sites, where the sources of capital control the terms and conditions of the entire private offering of securities.

The reason for this continuity is that most of the 25 newer websites are still exclusively focused on startup ventures. Once a company is operational, and generating top line sales revenue, the investment prospects for hitting the homerun are greatly diminished because there is no clear exit path for the investors to take a rapid capital gain.

Of the 25 CrowdFunding websites reviewed in Diagram 9, about 15 follow the traditional angel model, with the focus on startup companies. Only about 10 of the 25 websites in America are based upon helping small operational companies raise capital.

The distinction, from the eyes of the investor, concerns the difference between a capital gain from a new venture, and dividends and interests payments from operational companies that can share revenues and profits through consistent sales revenues.

Understanding the crucial distinction at the beginning of the capital raise between the traditional route and the newer internet CrowdFunding model means that the CEO of the company must prepare the entire private offering, prior to making a public solicitation for investors.

In the older method, now designated Reg D Rule 506(b), the company CEO can continue to go to the individual angels or venture capital firms, who would continue to set the terms and conditions, and prepare all the offering documents. Under the older method, there is no reason for the company to engage in sales and marketing to find investors, under Rule 506(c), if the company can find the investors in the venture capital community.

In Diagram 10, generally the websites designated as targeting startups or new ventures are more consistent with the earlier model of raising capital.

Diagram 10. Overview of U. S. Accredited and Non-Accredited CrowdFunding Websites

Name of Website	Description	URL	Stage	Investor
AngelList	Online feature lets accredited investors put small amounts of money into startups.	www.angel.co	Startups	Accredited
Blaze Fund Launch date August, 2013	Equity-based CrowdFunding platform	www.blazefund.com	Technology and business services ventures for a minimum raise of $100K	Accredited
CircleUp	Equity-based CrowdFunding platform	www.circleup.com	Consumer and retail companies	Accredited
Cofolio Launch date January, 2011	Allows small businesses to efficiently raise money from their local community.	www.mycofolio.com	Any small business that is looking for expansion capital	Non-accredited investors with a substantive, pre-existing relationship Accredited investors
CrowdFunder	Platform to get funding	www.crowdfunder.com	Film Entertainment Small Business Social Enterprise Tech Startup	41,688 investors
EarlyShares Launch date November, 2011	Equity CrowdFunding platform	www.EarlyShares.com	Companies with proprietary technology or other intellectual property and a sizeable market for its product or service	Accredited
EquityNet Launch date December, 2005	Equity CrowdFunding platform	www.equitynet.com	Any company in any stage or type of private businesses (from pre-revenue start-ups to $100M/yr in revenue	Features over 12,000 individual accredited investors
FundWisdom	Equity CrowdFunding platform	www.fundwisdom.com	Not stated	Accredited

FairStreet Launch date December, 2012	Community funding platform	www.fairstreet.com	Any small business qualifies to be listed on FairStreet once approved.	Accredited
Fundable Launch date May, 2012	Funding platform for startups	www.fundable.com	Startups	Accredited
FundersClub	Online venture funds with investment sizes typically ranging from $1K to $250K.	www.thefundersclub.com	Startup	Accredited
FundRoom	Social network that will link all parties needed to create and launch a successful venture.	www.fundroom.com	Not stated	Not stated
Go4Funding	Online platform that brings together entrepreneurs, investors, and business experts from around the world.	www.go4funding.com	Startups or established companies	Angel investor, private investor or venture capitalist
Healthfundr	Allows accredited investors to easily get to know and invest in early- to growth-stage, health and medtech companies.	www.healthfundr.com	Companies developing solutions to the toughest health issues	Accredited. investment minimums as low as $2,500.
IBanker Direct	Platform for accredited investors	www.ibankersdirect.com	Small-cap growth companies	Accredited
Invertual	Web 2.0 platform that brings together investors and investment groups entrepreneurs and businesses seeking capital	www.invertual.com	Not stated	Not stated
InvestorBillboard	Web portal will help our quality investors and startups connect	www.investorbillboard.com	Direct investment in small businesses.	Not stated
Localstake Launch date September, 2011	Locally focused CrowdFunding marketplaces that connect businesses seeking capital to local investors and community partners	www.localstake.com	Local businesses that are currently generating revenue. Under $1,000,000 in funding	Not stated, but appears to be oriented to non-accredited because of the cap on funding target.
Micro-funding Launch date December, 2006	Help early-stage startups raise funds from micro-investors.	www.micro-funding.com	Startups	Venture capital firms
MicroVentures	MicroVentures reviews startups in a process similar to other Venture Capital companies	www.microventures.com	Businesses likely to turn a profit within one to three years. Healthcare and the life sciences	Accredited

61

Poliwogg	Internet-based broker-dealer/crowd-funding portal/asset manager	www.poliwogg.com	Early stage companies in health and life sciences	Accredited
RockThePost Launch date November, 2011	Online investment platform that connects high quality entrepreneurs with investors	www.rockthepost.com	Startups	Accredited
SeedInvest Launch date April, 2012	Equity CrowdFunding platform	www.SeedInvest.com	Startups	Accredited
ZacksDirect Private	Provides a full suite of marketing communications and provides investors with access to research	www.zacksdirect.com	All Reg D companies	Accredited
The Private Capital Market Website is owned by Laurie Thomas Vass	Equity and debt accredited investor CrowdFunding platform	www.privatecapitalmarket.com	Startups and established technology companies	Accredited

Of the 10 accredited investor websites that target operational companies, three or four are more oriented to non-accredited investors, and are waiting for the final rules for Title III of the JOBS Act to be issued. Most of these websites also tend to focus on startups.

That leaves about six accredited investor CrowdFunding websites that focus on established companies.

These six websites are listed in Diagram 11.

Diagram 11. Overview of Six Accredited Investor Websites That Focus on Operational Companies

CircleUp	Equity-based CrowdFunding platform	www.circleup.com	Consumer and retail companies	Accredited
EarlyShares Launch date November, 2011	Equity CrowdFunding platform	www.EarlyShares.com	Companies with proprietary technology or other intellectual property and a sizeable market for its product or service	Accredited
EquityNet Launch date December, 2005	Equity CrowdFunding platform	www.equitynet.com	Any company in any stage or type of private businesses (from pre-revenue start-ups to $100M/yr in revenue	Features over 12,000 individual accredited investors
Go4Funding	Online platform that brings together entrepreneurs, investors, and business experts from around the world.	www.go4funding.com	Startups or established companies	Angel investor, private investor or venture capitalist
IBanker Direct	Platform for accredited investors	www.ibankersdirect.com	Small-cap growth companies	Accredited
The Private Capital Market Website is owned by Laurie Thomas Vass	Equity and debt accredited investor CrowdFunding platform	www.privatecapitalmarket.com	Startups and established technology companies	Accredited

Zack's Direct Private did not get placed on this list. While Zack's Direct Private has the appearance of an accredited investor website, it is actually more like a traditional public relations firm that offers marketing services to other websites or to individual companies that would like to tap into the large accredited investor database that is maintained by Zack's Research.

As they note on their website, "We are a full-service advertising agency focused on helping our clients communicate with investors. We provide a full suite of marketing services to suit any reasonable budget from template-based communications to custom solutions that are tailored to reach a specific pool of investors. Zack's Direct provides a full suite of marketing communications and provides investors with access to research."

The functionality of the other six websites can be compared in terms of the services that they offer to established operational companies.

For example, CircleUp, is a website operated by CircleUp Network, Inc. As they state on their website, "All securities related activity is conducted through Fundme Securities LLC, a wholly owned subsidiary of CircleUp Network, Inc. Fundme Securities LLC is a registered Broker/Dealer and member FINRA/SIPC."

As a FINRA broker-dealer, CircleUp is regulated by both the 1933 Securities Act and the 1934 Securities Market Act.

For a company raising CrowdFunding capital, the significance of this dual regulatory structure is that CircleUp's functionality is governed by the common law of agency, which means that the website staff and brokers of CircleUp are agents of their principal, Fundme Securities, which means that the agents owe their allegiance and loyalty to their principal.

The agents are bound by FINRA rules that direct the agents to "know their customers," meaning their investor clients. This regulatory framework places CircleUp more in the traditional venture capital business model, where the goal is to obtain a fast capital gain exit for their investor customers.

In their business model, traditional venture capital firms and angel partnerships funnel the company prospects into CircleUp, and provide initial screening and review of the companies that are seeking capital.

As CircleUp notes on its website, "We target companies that are positioned for investment or buyout by a larger brand or a private equity firm down the road."

Like the earlier venture capital model, the CircleUp model has a pre-existing set of investors, as clients, that the company is able to prospect to raise capital. As they note on their website, "CircleUp has a large community of accredited investors, many of whom have deep market experience, either as successful entrepreneurs giving back, or are people who love investing in the next generation of consumer businesses."

Companies that use CircleUp to raise capital are prohibited from doing sales and marketing to promote their listing, and drive potential investors to their listing on CircleUp, As they note on their site, "You are currently NOT allowed to make public announcements about your listing. This includes sending out mass emails and posting about the fundraising to social networks (e.g. Facebook, Twitter)."

In other words, the population of existing investors on the CircleUp platform are likely going to be the only investors who would have a reason to know about the company listing, much like the earlier venture capital model where only a select group of investors had knowledge of a company that was raising capital.

Like the earlier angel matching websites, the CircleUp model allows a company to list its offering on the CircleUp platform, but the company remains passive in terms of selecting the investors who choose to make an investment in the company.

As CircleUp notes on its website, "You are able to set a minimum investment amount per investor, but you are not able to seek out specific investors or limit your fundraising to a specific group of investors. Investments on CircleUp are open to the entire CircleUp community and are funded on a first come, first serve basis. Basically, investors who are excited about your company have a right to invest in it."

To summarize, CircleUp is built upon the earlier venture capital/angel model, but uses the functionality of the internet to list a company, much like the earlier angel matching websites. Of the six CrowdFunding websites listed in Diagram 10, two other websites follow a version of the CircleUp model.

A contrast with the CircleUp model is the CrowdFunding platform managed by I-Banker Direct. From the I-Banker had been in the business of providing intermediary market services to institutional investors since 1996, and began migrating towards a CrowdFunding business model around 2011.

The I-Bankers Direct web platform is designed to provide accredited investors with online access to the same types of investment opportunities that they had previously provided exclusively to institutional investors.

The difference in the history and experience between I-Banker and CircleUp explains much about how their two CrowdFunding platforms function for companies. In the case of CircleUp, their history was more in the angel/venture capital model and their evolution ended up being based upon that earlier experience.

I-Banker began life more as an investment banker, packaging deals between companies and big investors, and ended up offering that same type of service to smaller retail accredited investors. The I-Banker platform allows private companies to connect both to individual accredited investors and a select group of institutions.

A part of their functionality for companies comes from the earlier history of venture capital forums by enabling investors to have online access to company presentations, management conference calls and offering documents for each company raising capital.

One commonality between CircleUp and I-Banker is their regulatory structure. As I-Banker notes, "there is a strong affiliation between I-Bankers Direct, LLC and I-Bankers Securities, Inc. All securities offered on this website are offered through I-Bankers Securities, Inc. ("IBS") through an arrangement with I-Bankers Direct. IBS is a registered broker/dealer and FINRA/SIPC member."

So, even though the functionality of the I-Banker platform, seen from the perspective of a private company, is more extensive than CircleUp, and incorporates a population of institutional buyers, the staff and brokers at I-Banker owe their allegiance to their principals at I-Bankers Securities, Inc.

In terms of control over the terms and conditions of the company offering, the I-Banker model allows more flexibility, but with a big price to pay by the company. As I-Banker notes, "I-Bankers Direct professionals will work with management to determine the most practical terms of the offering. Companies raising capital through our portal will have established the terms of the offering prior to being listed on the portal."

As a part of the I-Banker model, it is an "all-or-nothing" proposition for the company. Either the company raises the entire target amount of capital, or the company gets nothing. As I-Banker notes, "If the target is not reached, all of the funds are promptly returned to the investor."

Unlike CircleUp, which prohibits a company from engaging in public marketing and promotion to attract investors, it appears as if I-Banker does not have this same type of prohibition against outside marketing by the company. Their website contains a link to the SEC proposed guidelines that highlight the Title II rules on public solicitation.

In order to compare the two FINRA broker dealer CrowdFunding platforms with a non-broker dealer accredited investor website, it is useful to examine EquityNet.

As EquityNet notes, "EquityNet is a web-based CrowdFunding platform. EquityNet is not a registered broker-dealer and does not offer investment advice or advise on the raising of capital through securities offerings."

In contrast to the two broker dealer platforms, which take a more "hands-on" approach to structuring a transaction, EquityNet takes a "hands-off" approach. "EquityNet takes no part in the negotiation or execution of transactions for the purchase or sale of securities, and at no time has possession of funds or securities. No securities transactions are executed or negotiated on or through the EquityNet platform. EquityNet receives no compensation in connection with the purchase or sale of securities."

Not being a broker dealer allows EquityNet to offer greater functionality to companies who would like to solicit investors using standardized document thats the company can obtain on the internet or in other marketing forums to seek potential investors.

As noted by EquityNet, in their company admin portal they have a "Funding" tab for the company profile that enables the company to market the offering.

As they note, there are already "hundreds" of accredited investors who use the EquityNet platform, and potential investors do not need to be a part of an angel group or have any prior affiliation of a broker dealer to register as a member of EquityNet to review private company offerings.

The greater flexibility in functionality for companies on EquityNet, compared to the two broker dealers, extends to how the investors conduct due diligence on the company, once the investors land on the EquityNet platform.

EquityNet offers an extensive set of unique patented technology software services that allows investors to efficiently screen and analyze thousands of investment opportunities in minutes. The company CEO can also use the screening software to screen and evaluate potential investors, and invite selected investors to examine the company's documents.

In other words, as a part of EquityNet's functionality, the screening software is a two-way street, which tends to make the ensuing capital transaction more of an equal exchange between buyers and sellers of capital.

To summarize, of the six accredited investor websites, two of them, CircleUp and I-Banker, are registered broker dealers, and one of them, EquityNet, is a subscription-based website. A type of hybrid CrowdFunding website that makes use of outside third parties to offer many services is EarlyShares.

EarlyShares has a partnership with both Crowdcheck and National Securities Corporation, a FINRA broker dealer.

Crowdcheck offers internet services to help investors conduct due diligence, and National Securities Corporation offers commission-based transaction and placement services for facilitating a transaction by an investor client of NSC into the private company.

In addition to making use of outside third party service providers, EarlyShares also allows both donor based giving to a company, and direct equity investments by accredited investors. It also mentions that at some point in the future, when Title III non-accredited investor rules are issued, that it will offer that function as well.

The EarlyShares "Posting Only" service offering is like a do-it-yourself service for the company CEO. EarlyShares provides, "all elements of the Offering – including the Legal Docs, Investment Terms, and Due Diligence – are the responsibility of the Issuer.

After launching the Offering and accepting one or more investor commitments, the Issuer posts the deal to the EarlyShares platform to enhance its visibility, reach additional investors, and conduct transactions. Posting Issuers must still complete the standard regulatory compliance and Due Diligence processes that accompany General Solicitation investment Offerings."

In the EarlyShares revenue model, companies pay a monthly posting fee and also pay a fee to the outside third party due diligence company, CrowdCheck.

Along the continuum of functionality and flexibility of CrowdFunding websites, the most company-centric website is Private Capital Market. As full and fair disclosure, Private Capital Market is owned by the author of this book, Laurie Thomas Vass. Vass developed the platform based upon his experience as an investment advisor representing the interests of small technology companies.

In other words, the prior experience for Private Capital Market was as an advisor to companies, while CircleUp and I-Banker were more influenced by their prior experience in the business world of venture capital and investment banking.

The prior experience between the six accredited investor websites explains most of the variation about their current services and offerings.

The biggest distinction about the Private Capital Market is that the website tends to see the process of raising capital from the eyes of the CEO, and grants the CEO maximum flexibility to conduct a direct corporate private offering.

In all six accredited investor CrowdFunding websites, the company CEO must perform certain tasks and duties to issue securities, prior to engaging in the offering. The new rules for Reg D Rule 506(c) make a distinction between the offering period and 60 days before an investor makes an actual investment in a company, and Chapter 5 addresses the tasks the company must perform to prepare to offer securities.

Chapter 6. Getting The Company Ready To Raise 506c CrowdFunding Capital

As mentioned in Chapter 2, raising capital with a CrowdFunding campaign is different for the CEO than the old model of going to different venture capital firms, seeking capital.

In CrowdFunding, the CEO, and the other senior executives, have more responsibility and duties in order to issue securities, especially in the six months prior to engaging in the offering. It may take as much as six months lead time to get the company ready to raise CrowdFunding, and then, another six months to conduct the offering.

About 80% of the lead time getting ready to issue securities is related to marketing and promoting the offering. In other words, much of the Rule 506c preparation involves organizing a marketing campaign to sell the securities. The marketing cost related to issuing the securities would be about $25,000.

Diagram 12. CEO Chronology of Tasks To Conduct a 506C Private Offering

Pre-Offering Period
Month 1
- Retain an Investment Advisor and read the Investment Advisor Disclosure Document and sign the Investment Advisor Agreement.
- If you need a business loan to finance the offering, select the loan partner.
- Select the securities attorney that prepares the offering documents. Assist the attorney in preparing all legal offering documents.
- Open 4 new outside vendor accounts:
EarlyIQ. Subscription fee due at registration.
Retain an internet marketing firm. Fill in the template to create the I nvestor Relations page.
Retain a back office custodian, like FundAmerica, or Folio Institutional.
- Modify the company website to add a new NAV button to the company page: News About Our Company, that contains full document uploads and videos about the offering that are linked to the short blurbs on the IR page.
- Prepare the company website to add a new NAV button for the Investor Relations page.
- Prepare 4 documents to upload into the new company "News About Us" page that are linked on the new Investor Relations page:
Quick Deal Overview.
Power Point Presentation.

Business Summary.
The Business Description Section of the Risk Disclosure Document

Month 2

- Create or modify company's social media pages to begin adding blogs about the company
  LinkedIn
  Face Book
  Twitter
  Google+
- Create the formal legal business buy sell agreement and fund it with insurance.
- Upload press releases and upcoming events to the new Investor Relations page.
- Begin writing press releases and establishing relationships with business media outlets.
- If you need to value the company, retain AlgoValue to run the valuation.
- Review all public and private competitors as comps to begin the process of valuing the company at AlgoValue.
- Place company profile on outside profile listing sites and solicit their investors.
  DealFlow.
  EquityNet.
  FinRoad (Europe)
  Fundable.
  The Funded.
  Zacks (free)

Month 3

- Begin searching for CEO events to present Power Point. Place the dates for events on company IR page.
- Begin creating the affiliate and affinity email contact lists.
- Select vendors for social media marketing and press release distribution.
- Select vendors for buying email lists and begin email marketing.
- Combine email marketing with outbound calling to arrange CEO calls to potential investors.
- Prepare initial company 5 minute video advertorial and one minute video ad and distribute the videos via MarketWired or Business Wire.
- Consider using Deal Flow blog advertising.

Offering Period
Month 4.
- Upload all offering documents onto company EarlyIQ's Room 506 deal room software.
- Upload Subscription Agreement onto company FundAmerica account page.
- Select FINRA brokers for securities sales distribution at FundAmerica, independents and Zacks.
- Implement Google Ad words and FaceBook ads. Fees apply for each service.
- Begin monthly email campaign to affiliates and affinity markets. Fees apply.
- Combine email marketing with outbound calling to arrange CEO calls to potential investors.
- Begin company CEO presentations and write a press release for each presentation.

Month 5
- Continue all marketing activities and answer investor questions about the process of making an investment.

Month 6
- Direct all investors to open investor escrow accounts at FundAmerica by following the Invest Now button from EarlyIQ.
- Advise investors to open a securities account at Folio, to hold book entry company securities after they are transferred by FundAmerica.
- Execute closing at FundAmerica and transfer capital to company securities account at Folio.

Month 7
- Create new Investor Relations page to communicate with investors after offering closes.
- Leave the FundAmerica account open to administer taxes and distributions to investors.

Post-Offering Period
Month 8.
- Prepare company securities for secondary exchanges and Alternative Trading Systems listings.

Month 9
- Begin monthly emails to all investors to update them on company progress.
- Initiate quarterly financial reporting on company IR page for access by investors.

The new rules for Reg D Rule 506c make a distinction between the time offering period starts and 60 days before an investor makes an actual investment in a company. The verification of the accredited investor's status is only valid for a period of 60 days, prior the actual transfer of capital from the investor to the company.

Most of the accredited investor verification process is outsourced to administrative firms, who charge about $50 per investor.

Unstated in the new rules are the tasks that must be performed the CEO prior to the start of a general public solicitation. In other words, in addition to the 60 days that the CEO has to confirm the credentials of a potential investor, and in addition to the time period that the securities offering begins, there is an additional six month period of time for the CEO to prepare the entire offering package of documents, called the offering documents.

Part of the preliminary management tasks of the offering involves getting the personal financial affairs of the CEO's family protected if the CEO dies, and part of the management involves insulating the family financial assets from civil claims against the CEO, or the company, if an aggrieved investor makes a claim, after securities have been issued.

To be clear, if everything in a future Reg D 506(c) ran perfectly, the CEO and all the senior executives of a company, would need to modify their estate plans because the new capital investments in the company change ownership interests and create new, unknown future liabilities and claims, both during the life, and after the death, of a CEO.

Diagram 13 describes the set of management tasks that the CEO and other senior executives need to perform to get the company ready to undertake CrowdFunding. The rest of this chapter explains more about what each task would entail.

The major change in the new way of accredited investor CrowdFunding capital, from the traditional venture capital method, is that there will not be a period of time for private negotiations between the company and different groups of investors, once the offering period begins because all potential investors must be treated uniformly and fairly.

It would not be uniform and fair treatment if one set of investors got terms and conditions that were different than the terms offered to other investors.

In the new method, the CEO will establish the terms and conditions of the investment prior to the beginning of the offering process. Once those terms and conditions have been established, then they must be maintained, in tact, throughout the offering period.

In order to avoid the allegation of fraud in a public solicitation, the company must prepare the terms and conditions of the offering before making public statements about the offering.

Otherwise, what is said by the executive in public to one set of investors may turn out to be a false representation, if the company changes the terms with a second set of investors, in private, non-public negotiations over the terms.Diagram 12. Outline of CEO

Diagram 13. Tasks To Get The Company Ready To Raise CrowdFunding Capital

Personal and Family Financial Tasks	Business and Professional Tasks
Coordinating family estate settlement plans with business ownership transition plans.	Implementing a company buy-sell legal agreement, funded by life insurance, compatible with the form of securities issued.
Coordinating family civil liability and trust arrangements with business liability and errors and omissions insurance.	Implementing company product and professional liability insurance before the securities are issued, and implementing a comprehensive company liability insurance policy, coordinated with Board of Director's liability insurance covering existing and new members of the Board.
Coordinating CEO retirement plans and exit strategy with executive compensation arrangements after securities have been issued.	Inserting the legal terms and conditions in new securities that protect the financial interests of the CEO.
	Working with the company securities attorneys to draft the set of offering documents.
	Working with the company securities attorneys to manage questions from investors about the documents.
	Working with the company securities attorneys to conduct the public solicitation within the rules for the new Reg D Rule 506(c) offering.
	Preparing the internet marketing strategy to attract investors and manage investor communications during and after the offering.
	Preparing the schedule of public presentations by the CEO during the offering, including internet webinars.
	Implementing internal company policies on public statements by senior managers during the offering.
	Working with the company CPA and other professional advisors on financial statements related to the public offering, consistent with the provisions for disclosure of financial condition.

After the terms and conditions have been revealed to one potential accredited investor, the same terms and conditions must be revealed to all potential accredited investors.

Getting the offering terms and subscription agreements right from the start has serious implications for the estate settlement plans of the owners of the companies. In other words, there is a critical nexus of financial and legal issues for the CEO between CrowdFunding and family estate settlement that the owners need to get right, before the CrowdFunding project begins.

The estate settlement plans of company executives will change as a result of CrowdFunding. Creating the will is the first step among many steps to take for making certain that assets and income are transferred to family members or to other beneficiaries, and that the technology company can continue to function after the death of the CEO or owner.

A will is a written declaration by an individual—called the testator—of his or her intentions for the disposition of assets after death. A local probate judge at the county courthouse will review the will and if everything seems correct, will order that the title to property named in the will is transferred to the beneficiary.

In other words, just like general warranty deed is used by the county clerk of court to transfer the legal ownership of real estate between buyer and seller, the probate court uses the will to execute the legal order to transfer ownership title of estate property to the beneficiaries named in the will.

The written declaration of intent must be prepared a long time before death, and the will must be updated every year by the technology firm owner to reflect changes in ownership interests in company property that is to be transferred.

The CEO, and each senior executive of the technology firm, must create a will, and one of the questions asked by the CEO every year at the annual company picnic is if the other senior managers have updated their will to reflect any changes in equity ownership or debt of the company related to the executive.

The reason for the annual review is that the new CrowdFunding rules contain "Bad Boy" provisions related to Dodd-Frank legislation.

Any person, in the entire chain of company authority, both inside and outside the company, related to a Reg D Rule 506(c) offering, must disclose their prior history of regulatory compliance, and all the Bad Boys must be excluded from the offering process.

If some event had arisen in the prior year, that the CEO or other owners had not been made aware of related to being a Bad Boy, then the CEO would need to know about that event, and the Bad Boy would need to amend their will to reflect a change in their ownership interests in the company.

This provision applies to Bad Girls, too.

The best idea is for the CEO to create and amend the will, before the company begins the CrowdFunding project, and to modify the parts of the will that may relate to the ownership interests in the company as a result of raising capital.

The will is the basic legal building block of estate settlement, and its terms affect all the other legal documents that may be created, like trusts, as a part of the estate settlement.

An important document that has a name similar to the probate will is called the "Living Will." Unlike the probate will, which describes intent to transfer property at death, the living will describes the desire of the person for health care in the period of time before death.

A living will is a document that allows people to specify the life-sustaining treatments they would find acceptable in the final days of terminal illness or incapacity. Forty-eight states and the District of Columbia have living-will laws (all states except Massachusetts and Michigan).

A legal document related to the living will is called the durable health care power of attorney, which grants a delegation of legal decision-making powers to another person..

The power of attorney gives the other person the ability to make decisions as if it was the person who granted the power.

It's durable because the power conveyed to the agent does not lapse if the principal becomes incompetent. In most cases, the durable power of attorney for health care provides for:
- The right to remove a physician
- The right to have the incompetent patient discharged against medical advice
- The right to medical records

- The right to have the patient moved
- The right to engage other treatment

If a person died without a valid will, he or she is said to have died intestate, and the probate court will distribute his or her property under the intestate succession statutes of the state, without any consideration for the decedent's unique personal situation.

The intestacy statutes only take into consideration family relationships; they do not take into account such factors as managing a company, taxes, administration costs, or estate shrinkage.

Without a will, it may be legally impossible to manage the company after the CEO dies because no person has the legal authority to make decisions for the business.

Even with a valid will, continual operation and administration of the company may be impossible if the company did not also have a legal document in place describing how the company would be managed if an owner died.

The best idea is to create a legal agreement, called a buy-sell agreement, to pass the ownership interests of the CEO to other partners or owners. The separate buy-sell agreement must be described in the will or there may be legal disputes about how the business property is managed or transferred after death.

Long before a company embarks on a CrowdFunding project, the CEO and all the other owners of the company need to modify their wills and amend their buy-sell agreements to reflect what happens during and after the investment of new capital into the company.

The priority of events in creating the two sets of documents would first be the creation of the family estate settlement legal documents, because those documents have many more options for moving the title of property and assets from one owner to another, both before and after someone dies.

Property rights are primarily a state issue, while accredited investor CrowdFunding is primarily a federal issue, so it is best to get the state property rights set first, in wills and trusts, and then deal with the federal issues of how CrowdFunding affects property rights and federal estate taxes.

The terms of the family estate settlement documents would refer to the terms and conditions in the second set of business documents related to the buy-sell agreements and the other corporate legal documents, (like the minutes and resolutions passed at Board meetings) and then, both sets of documents (family and business), would be reviewed for conformity and consistency with the new CrowdFunding rules, because CrowdFunding has legal implications on how company ownership changes when capital is added to a company.

CrowdFunding creates legal rights and possible claims of the new CrowdFunding investors against the estate of the CEO. In addition to that set of claims, the existing owners and early round investors may also have claims and grievances against the new CrowdFunding investors. And, family members and family beneficiaries may have claims against both sets of investors.

The first priority in coordinating estate settlement with CrowdFunding is to segregate the transfer of business property owned by the CEO from oversight of the probate court, when the CEO dies. The main idea here is to involve one less judge in the estate settlement process involving the on-going management of the company.

As an issue of property law in most states, properties the grantor (owner/CEO) transfers to the revocable living trust during life are not subject to probate at the grantor's death. Thus, assets, such as the CEO's shares in the company, can be placed in a trust to avoid the delays and the costs of settling or probating an estate. Probate costs, probate time, and probate claims may be substantial.

A trust acts like a unique corporation, with its own imaginary life existence. As the title suggests, a trust involves a lot of trust between the creator of the trust (trustor and CEO) and the beneficiaries of the trust (beneficiaries) and the administrator of the trust (trustee).

The CEO creates the trust, and then places her ownership interests into the trust before she dies, and a long time before she starts the CrowdFunding project. Putting her shares of the company in the trust helps to avoid having those ownership interests subjected to review by a probate judge because the title of the shares passes directly to the legal control of the trustee.

In the absence of a trust to place the shares, the local probate court judge would appoint an estate executor who will collect all the properties of the estate, and hold these properties under the jurisdiction of the probate court until creditors' claims are satisfied and other formalities of death, including taxes, are complied with.

Then, when the estate legal issues have been resolved, the executor will distribute the remaining properties as directed in the decedent's will.

If the company owed money to suppliers, or had bank lines of credit, then the executor would direct that estate assets be used to pay those debts.

Until those business debts are cleared, the management and administration of the company will be in limbo because only the executor can make legal decisions about the business during the estate settlement period.

This management limbo applies to securities that may have been bought by investors during a previous CrowdFunding project.

During this estate settlement time, which usually ranges from six months to a year or more, the estate assets may be poorly invested and income or principal may not be readily available to the beneficiaries or heirs. The probate court is not under any obligation to select an executor who knows how to run a business.

The revocable living trust can be especially important if the grantor owns business or real estate property in states other than the state of his residence. The grantor can avoid multiple probate proceedings in several states (called ancillary probate) by legally re-titling the shares and placing them in the trust during the life of the CEO.

In the case of business ownership shares of the CEO, the trust document would authorize the trustee to sell the shares that had been placed in the trust to other buyers, such as the other owners of the company.

When the trustee obtained the cash from the sale of the shares, the trustee would be obligated to use the proceeds to provide income and benefits to the beneficiaries of the trust, usually the spouse or children of the CEO.

The creation and execution of the trust must be coordinated with the other legal documents involving the business interests held by the CEO, including the value of the securities owned by the CEO that may have been issued under CrowdFunding that are held in the trust.

The new wrinkle in CrowdFunding for valuing shares is that the CEO and the other senior managers involved in CrowdFunding set the terms and conditions of the securities, including their price when the new investors buy them.

While the shares previously issued in CrowdFunding do not go through the probate court, if they had been placed in a trust before death, the shares are includable in the valuation of the CEO's estate.

In the older venture capital method, the venture capitalists and investment bankers set the terms and conditions, including the price of the securities. The price established by the venture capitalists may not have been the most advantageous to the CEO in valuing the shares, especially in the case of estate valuation.

Under IRC Section 2703, a business buy-sell agreement must be:
- A bona fide business arrangement
- Not a device to transfer property to family members for less than full and adequate consideration
- Be comparable in its terms to those entered into by persons in arm's length transactions
- Must prohibit an individual owner from selling his or her interest during life without first offering it to the business or to the other owners at the price specified in the agreement

Presumably, if the CEO complied with Section 2703, but subject to review by legal counsel, the value of shares set by the CEO for CrowdFunding securities would be legitimate evidence of a bona fide business arrangement that could be used to place a value on the shares that are bought from the trust, when the CEO dies.

As described in Chapter 10, the new CrowdFunding rules increase the risk for CEOs related to committing fraud in any part of an investment offering.

The new increased risk arises from the CEO making a mistake in the offering. The mistake creates potential claims against the estate of the CEO, if the CEO happens to die within one year of the close of the Reg D offering.

The one year period is related to new rules on the rights of rescission of investors who may have made an investment, under an exemption granted to the company under Reg D Rule 506(c), if that exemption is subsequently revoked because the CEO made a mistake.

If a CEO makes a mistake, and the exemption is revoked, then all the investors (not just the unqualified purchaser) have the right to rescind or cancel its purchase and recover the purchase price (plus interest) from the issuer for one year after the sale.

One part of the solution for making a mistake occurs six months before the offering period begins. The CEO and senior managers involved with the offering need to be covered by company-owned errors and omissions insurance, and also professional liability insurance that covers the act of issuing securities.

In addition to the company-owned insurance, the executives should also buy individually-owned liability insurance related to their management roles with the company.

The insurance solution does not solve the legal issues of making a mistake, it only tends to indemnify the executives from financial loss related to the mistake.

If any of the senior executives also serve on the company board of directors, then they should have individually-named insured status on the company-owned Directors and Officers liability policy, in place well in advance of the period of time the offering begins.

As a second partial strategy for dealing with the consequences of a mistake, the CEO can work with the estate attorney to create a third legal instrument, called a family limited partnership, (FLP). The strategy described is primarily intended for what is commonly called a "growth equity" company, where the CEO intends to own and manage a successful company for an indefinite period of time.

The premise of the FLP estate strategy is that Title II accredited investor CrowdFunding will be used when the investment goal for CrowdFunding investors is primarily in the form of ongoing dividends and interest from the securities, with the rights to convert to equity, if the company is sold.

Existing stockholder rights make a growth equity investment more complex to structure and negotiate with the issuance of stock. In a debt offering, the negative covenants or veto rights to block company issuances of additional debt or equity securities, particularly equity securities with equal or more senior liquidation preferences, are the more relevant factors for growth equity investors.

This relationship between company insurance and estate planning is one of the benefits of using the Family Limited Partnership in relation to a CrowdFunding capital raise.

Each share or ownership interest in a CrowdFunding would bear a stamped red ink restriction on the future transfer or assignment, no matter who or what investor bought the CrowdFunding securities.

In the case of the CEO's ownership interests, the shares would be restricted and linked to the estate settlement strategy.

In the case of the CEO who created an FLP, the first right of refusal to buy shares would be in favor of the company or the other owners of the company. The next right of refusal would be for the FLP, or members of the FLP.

A family limited partnership (FLP) is a business and financial planning device that can combine business operational planning, personal tax planning, transfer of family wealth, and business succession planning, all under one flexible arrangement.

The family limited partnership is a real life operating company, which attempts to make a profit at running a family-owned business. Unlike the imaginary life of a trust, that lies dormant during the life of the CEO, the family limited partnership has real people who manage the operations and assets of the business, during the life of the CEO, which could be a family farm, a real estate development firm, or a private technology company.

The FLP does not necessarily have any management oversight of the technology business of the CEO, but more likely, the FLP manages a related business, such as the real estate business that rents the building or lab space to the technology company.

The CEO must decide whether there is a family member or heir who is willing and able to run the FLP business.

If such individuals are not available, the FLP may identify a key employee or related person from the technology company, to manage the FLP.

Shares of the ownership of an FLP interest may be held by any natural person or legal entity, and a FLP may have an unlimited number of partners.

One of the important business functions of the FLP is to manage the technology company ownership transfer process immediately after the sudden death of the CEO. In other words, in the period of time immediately following the death, the FLP provides management continuity and estate transfer services to the family and the company.

The FLP is not an irrevocable arrangement, and allows plenty of "elbow room" if changes become necessary, as a result of accredited investor CrowdFunding.

At the death of the CEO, the crowdfunded shares owned by the technology company CEO will be valued for the CEO's estate tax purposes, and that price per share value will affect the value of all other shareholders who own the affected securities.

The CEO is primarily responsible for setting the price per share at the beginning of the CrowdFunding project. The estimated value of the securities must be maintained by the CEO throughout the offering period.

In the years after the offering, for estate planning purposes, and for business buy-sell agreements, the estimated value of the securities should be updated every year.

To summarize, the estate planning steps to take, before a CrowdFunding strategy is implemented, involve three legal documents: a will, a trust, and a family limited partnership, all of which are tied together by a fourth legal document called a "funded buy-sell agreement."

The CEO's will and trust documents will be more extensive than the other FLP partners because the CEO's estate settlement documents refer to both the legal agreements in the technology company and to the FLP legal doscuments, which are both linked together by the terms of the buy-sell agreement.

The term "funded" means that the buy-sell agreements in the technology company and the FLP partnership documents authorize the technology company and the FLP to apply for, buy, own and pay the premiums on life insurance on the life of the CEO.

For the technology company, the buy-sell agreement is a binding legal document that mandates that the ownership interests of the technology company held in the estate are bought from the estate and transferred to other owners, at the agreed upon price per share.

The FLP articles of incorporation and by-laws authorize the FLP to acquire a policy on the CEO, in her capacity as a member of the FLP. Upon that CEO's death, the death benefit insurance proceeds pour into the FLP, where they may be used to purchase assets or make loans to the estate of the deceased partner CEO.

Through this use of insurance death benefits, the estate of the CEO secures the cash it needs to help pay death taxes and other estate settlement costs, including the costs of keeping the technology company solvent.

The life insurance death benefits generally flow through to the surviving FLP partners as income-tax-free life insurance proceeds. The death benefit proceeds are used to buy the ownership interests at a step up in cost basis for the survivor's units that are bought from the estate.

In other words, the CEO's FLP can buy and own life insurance on the CEO's life, and also on the new outside Title II accredited investors who may have ownership interests in the technology company. The life insurance policies owned by the FLP must have a reasonable business purpose and be owned by an FLP that has an independent or reasonable business purpose, such as managing the real estate assets of the technology company. The FLP organizational document must authorize the FLP to buy and own life insurance.

The amount of death proceeds includable in CEO's estate will be a pro rata amount proportionate to his or her retained percentage interest. For example, a 2% ownership interest in the FLP by the CEO would mean that 2% of the life insurance death proceeds received by the FLP would be included in the gross estate of the CEO.

Both the FLP, in its capacity as a legal tax-paying entity, and the technology company, will apply for, pay for, and own life insurance on the life of the CEO, and perhaps also on the lives of other key executives. The legal language in all the documents, including the life insurance policies, will describe that only the FLP, or the technology company, are the legal owners of the life insurance, and that the CEO has no incidents of ownership in the life insurance, or legal control over how the death benefits are distributed.

The life insurance owned by the FLP permits the CEO to reduce the value of her estate without losing control of the technology company assets, including any ownership interests in the technology company that have been gifted or sold to other members of the FLP.

The life insurance on the CEO that is owned by the technology company pays out a death benefit directly to the company, which is then used to buy the shares away from the members of the family FLP, or from the estate of the CEO, for any shares that were not transferred to the FLP before death.

The ownership interests or securities issued to Title II accredited investors in the CrowdFunding project will have those securities restricted in the legal offering documents, and those restrictions on transfer will be coordinated with both the buy-sell agreements and the FLP legal language about how the technology company is managed if one of the CrowdFunding investors dies.

Either the company, or the FLP, is legally obligated to buy the shares from the accredited investor's estate, and the investor's estate is legally obligated to sell, at the pre-determined price per share.

During the life of the CEO, the FLP and the technology company each pay the premiums on the life insurance, and the life insurance builds up cash value inside the policy.

The cash value during the life of the CEO is described as a cash asset on the balance sheet of either the FLP or the company.

During the life of the CEO, the CEO's ownership interests in the technology company are contributed to the FLP in exchange for a partnership interests, and no gain or loss is recognized to the contributing partner or the partnership. After the ownership interests have been transferred to the FLP, the FLP makes a distribution of ownership interests to the other FLP family members.

The CEO's tax basis in the partnership interest is the adjusted basis of property contributed by the CEO to the FLP, plus any money contributed to the FLP, for example, cash used to pay operating expenses of the FLP.

Where the CEO's partnership interest is subsequently bequeathed and inherited by other FLP members, through the will or through the trust agreements, the initial basis is the fair market value of the technology company shares on the CEO's date of death or the alternate valuation date.

If the partnership interest is acquired by gift, during the life of the CEO, the initial basis of the interest is the donor's adjusted basis plus any gift tax paid by the donor.

The securities laws involved with a Reg D Rule 506 (c) offering are intertwined with the legal issues of protecting the CEO's personal financial affairs.

The securities laws require that the CEO provide all investors with full, fair and complete disclosure of all material facts about the company. Some of the disclosures may involve revealing personal financial information about the senior executives, and disclosure of business agreements between owners. Whatever information is revealed to one potential investor must be revealed to all potential investors.

Within six months of beginning a Reg D Rule 506 (c) offering, both the company and the personal tax records of the executives should be reviewed by an independent CPA to make certain that no negative disclosures, including liens and bankruptcies must be made in any of the offering materials.

If the company intends on issuing debt or obtaining financing from a commercial lender, than the personal financial statements of the owners should be prepared and audited, within six months of beginning the offering.

In addition, within 6 months of beginning an accredited investor CrowdFunding project, the company balance statement must be audited. This information about the company balance sheet could be provided in separate materials, such as a private placement memo, but if the information is given to any single potential investor, then the same information must be given to all accredited investors.

More information about the risks and liabilities of offering securities are in Chapter 10, but six months prior to beginning an offering, the CEO should prepare documents and materials that describe the company, its business operations, the members of its management team and any other material facts related to the company, including a review by an independent attorney of the status of any "bad boys and girls" that could possibly be related to the offering.

The materials should also set forth a description of risk factors related to a potential investment in the company. Examples of risk factors include a description of the company's operating history; risks related to the industry in which the company operates; risks specific to the company's products, technologies or services; and the risk that the investors may lose their entire investment in the company.

The new provisions of Reg D Rule 506 (c) contain disclosure legends that must be placed on all offering materials. Prior to starting an offering, all the risks should be used as the content and materials that guide the creation of power point presentations and webinars related to promoting the offering, and once a set of disclosures has been agreed upon by the CEO and the outside legal securities advisors, then that set of information must be maintained throughout the offering period by all executives involved with the offering.

Chapter 7. Selling Private Securities: The New Internet Pull Marketing

Pull marketing means using internet marketing tools to attract potential accredited investors to begin a relationship with the company. The CEO uses marketing tools to pull in the investors, primarily from outside websites on the internet.

The potential new investor is alerted to the investment opportunity, and uses the CEO's link on the internet to navigate to the company website to find out more information about the company. The CEO pulls them in to land on the company website, or an independent CrowdFunding portal, by using key words and text that the potential investor may be searching.

Pull marketing has both a social media component and an important regulatory component that is often overlooked in media reports on the new rules for Reg D Rule 506(c). The older regulatory component concerns how the investor found out about the company. The establishment of the pre-existing relationship is somewhat related to the set of FINRA regulations that guide the sales behavior of stock brokers.

The guiding polar star for brokers is to "Know Your Customer." The main regulatory logic of the Know Your Customer rule is that if you know your customer, you will not sell her unsuitable investments, for your own financial gain.

A version of this logic applies to CrowdFunding. A CEO would want to know their investor before the investor made an investment in the company. If the CEO knows her investor, then the CEO will not accept investment capital from an unsuitable investor.

However, the application of the rule for CEOs is a little bit different than Know Your Customer rule for stock brokers because in CrowdFunding, the regulatory burden of confirming the credentials of the potential investor shifted to the shoulders of the CEO.

The burden of proof is on the company CEO to document how they managed the process of a private offering in a way that allowed all investors uniform and fair access to all material facts about the offering. This burden follows a historical continuity in the law originating with a 1953 U. S. Supreme Court decision that companies must provide sufficient information to allow accredited investors to "fend for themselves."

In the 1953 Supreme Court decision, (U.S. Supreme Court, SEC v. Ralston Purina Co., 346 U.S. 119 (1953)), the majority ruled that, "Since exempt transactions are those as to which "there is no practical need for. . . [the bill's] application," the applicability of § 4(1) should turn on whether the particular class of persons affected need the protection of the Act. An offering to those who are shown to be able to fend for themselves is a transaction "not involving any public offering."

In that case, the Court highlighted full and fair disclosure of all information to investors who had the experience and knowledge to evaluate the merits of the offering. As the Court ruled, " But, once it is seen that the exemption question turns on the knowledge of the offerees, the issuer's motives, laudable though they may be, fade into irrelevance."

The Court stated that if the private placement offer had been made to those qualified investors, who because of their position, had access to the same kind of information that an SEC-registered offer would have disclosed, then the offer would be considered private and exempt from registration.

The accredited investor rules continue that historical application of providing information to qualified investors who are able to fend for themselves. The new wrinkle in the Reg D Rule 506(c) rules is that the burden of demonstrating the adequacy of information that has been disclosed to investors shifts to the CEO.

In pull marketing, part of the documentary evidence of full disclosure for the CEO is related to the issue of how the investor learned about the company, and began the "pre-existing" relationship, as an accredited investor. That type of evidentiary trail begins by having the potential investor land on the company website to begin due diligence about the company.

The new social media techniques of pull marketing solve much of the CEO's dilemma for compliance with both the new CrowdFunding rules and the older "fend-for-yourself" rules. Before the private company engages in a CrowdFunding private capital offer, the owners of the company can use the new tools of internet social media to initiate conversations with investors, who self-select themselves into their pre-existing relationship with the company.

The first new social media tool for finding accredited investors is the creation of an investor relations page on a multi-functional company website, that allows users and visitors to comment on the products and services of the company. In this phase of social media marketing, the relationship is about the company itself, and not about any offer, or even a hint of a potential offer of securities.

The investor relations page on the company website, in other words, is social media website that connects to popular social media sites like LinkedIn or Twitter.

The CEO uses those other websites to pull in potential investors to land on the company website. The company website is enabled as a blog, with its own unique name that is related to, or suggests, the name of the CEO. The blog is not just about the company or the product or services that the company sells.

The blog is also about the owner, because in social media, personal, non-business, news and information about the CEO is interesting to the wider internet community.

As an added benefit, in addition to the blog, the company website may also be e-commerce ready, with its own shopping cart and payment portals. When potential investors land on the site, they may comment on products that they have already purchased, and may decide to buy more, once they are on the site. They may offer testimonials, or add a "like" on Facebook, which may attract other viewers.

Videos and web cams can also be enabled on the company website because videos are a big part of the new social media pull marketing. The CEO may consider appearing in videos, or company webinars, which are archived on the company website, and distributed to outside websites, like YouTube, to pull in potential investors.

The main idea about using social media to find potential accredited investors is that the user sees the personal side of the CEO first, and then may decide to go to the company fan page to see about the products and services. Using social media implies that the CEO must actually read and engage in conversations with other people, and figure out what they like, and respond to them, just like the CEO would do if she met the person in a face-to-face business social networking event or meeting.

In other words, the CEO uses social media to offer relevant information that "pulls-them-in" to engage in a conversation, which eventually ends up establishing the pre-existing relationship. Much later, after a private offering has begun, the potential investor may be asked to describe how they first learned of the company, and how they established their "pre-existing" relationship.

The new social media marketing to find investors can be categorized as either affinity or affiliation marketing, both of which have a regional geographical component.

Recent research by Xuan Tian, conducted at the Kelley School of Business, Indiana University (2009), suggests that most private companies raised capital within 25 miles of the company.

While his research was more focused on the legal structure of the terms and conditions of capital investment, (Chapter 7), his findings are relevant to finding accredited investors. What he found was that local investors tended to have greater loyalty and allegiance, with closer geographical proximity and that the legal structure of the offering tended to be "company-friendly," the closer the company was located to the investor. In social media, users are searching the internet for knowledge and information that they find useful or interesting.

The CEO uses social media to attract the users, using terms and language that the users are searching for. Part of social media pull marketing is about knowledge creation and diffusion about the company.

Much of the knowledge diffusion about the company has a local characteristic because users are searching for knowledge that enhances their own knowledge, where they live.

In marketing research conducted by Pierre Desrochers, (Proximity and the Transmission of Tacit Knowledge, (The Review of Austrian Economics: 14:1: 25-46: 2001), Desrochers noted that, "...geographic concentration of economic activity is explained, among other factors by the importance of geography in the transmission of tacit knowledge... there is thus much evidence pointing toward the importance of geographical proximity for communication between people sharing a "common cognitive ground," it seems obvious that its importance is even greater for people possessing diverse backgrounds."

"Yet the essence of innovation," states Desrochers, "is the combination of previously unrelated knowledge and the collaboration of individuals possessing previously unrelated types of knowledge." The CEO is using terms and language that possess the knowledge that the internet user is searching for, and "invites" the user to learn more, in a form of social media collaboration.

As explained by Desrochers," the collaboration occurs as a result of close geographical proximity by allowing certain individuals better opportunities to tap into tacit knowledge than individuals located elsewhere." Part of the knowledge is shared knowledge about technology and potential investment opportunities.

In other words, CrowdFunding provides the communication platform that allows for a synchronous search by the CEO and potential investors, which potentially could lead to a private capital market exchange.

Ola Bengtsson and S. Abraham Ravid surveyed of 1800 private firms that raised capital, (The Geography of Venture Capital Contracts, SSRN, 2009). They found that VCs prefer to invest in companies that are located close to where the VC lives.

About 32% of all companies raised their capital from investors located within 10 miles of the lead VC, and 42% of companies were located no more than 50 miles from the lead VC.

The main point for social media CrowdFunding success relates to the importance of regional culture and customs. "Our results are confirm that differences in contract design that refer to regional culture and customs," they state. Of interest for CrowdFunding is that the closer the proximity between the company and the investor, the more "company-friendly" the terms and conditions were.

The most important change in understanding social media for an accredited investor CrowdFunding strategy is that potential investors are using the internet to find information that improves their decision making, not necessarily looking for the lowest cost item. At the beginning of their search, the potential investor is probably not aware that an investment opportunity exists, and may not be searching for a financial or investment relationship.

What this first change in pull marketing means for CrowdFunding is that the CEO must anticipate that potential investors are searching for longer term knowledge, not a relationship based on a quick price based encounter.

Attempting to use internet marketing to conduct a CrowdFunding project, without first understanding why potential investors are using the internet, or where they may be on the internet when they first discover the company, will result in a failed effort.

The second big change for pull marketing in a CrowdFunding project is based on a change from one directional messaging in the old venture capital model to multiple channels and two-way communication on the internet. The information exchange is a two-way communication between users and information flows across different modes, or pathways, such as instant messaging, internet connected tv, emails and smart phones.

Once information about the company is posted, or uploaded to a website, the text of the blog, or a user review, becomes a historically permanent piece of information on the internet that other users may rely upon to guide decisions. The influence and impact of the blog or review permanently alters the user's perception of the information about the company.

What this second change means for CEOs is that they must anticipate ongoing information exchanges with potential investors and be prepared to have conversations over an extended period of time. In pull marketing, the messages are sent before, during, and after the investment transaction occurs.

A third big change for CrowdFunding marketing is related to the distinction between linear and non-linear messages. In the older advertising and public relations model, the images were packaged along a linear communication path. For example, a radio, television, or newspaper ad for a seller contained a one-way path to increase the awareness of the viewer and shape perceptions.

For CrowdFunding, this third change means that the CEO will engage the potential investors in many different markets and respond to inquiries when the users want feedback, Potential investors will find news and information about the company, and will search for the CEO along different pathways. The CEO must set up the pull marketing management system that mirrors the way users will communicate with the company.

The main point for a CEO contemplating a pull marketing CrowdFunding project is that the marketing strategy to find investors will be an extended, open, ongoing offer to potential investors, inviting them to imagine their future relationship with the company.
Helping potential accredited investors "imagine" having a relationship with the company can be broken into 4 distinct tasks:
- Helping the user find the company on the Internet.
- Helping the user imagine having a relationship with the company by describing how the relationship "fits" into the user's individual (affiliation marketing) or social welfare function (affinity marketing).
- Helping the potential investor "actualize" the relationship by making it very easy for the user to conduct an investigation of the potential benefits of the relationship.
- Establishing an ongoing user feedback communication mechanism for an information exchange based upon the mutual benefits of the relationship.

In a rough approximation, these four steps fit into the theory of social exchange developed by Kelly and Thibaut in their social exchange theory.

Applied to CrowdFunding, their work suggests analyzing relationships before, during, and after an exchange in o continues to influence each other after the exchange.
In the case of using the internet for CrowdFunding, the internet constitutes the technological platform for facilitating the the behavior of the company and potential investor continues to affect each other's behavior after a private capital investment transaction.

In the case of CrowdFunding, the CEO is interested in finding potential investors in two different markets on the internet:
- the affinity market of internet users who share an interest with other internet users, and
- the affiliate market of users who have some potential financial interest in the survival of the company.

Economists have a term for expressing the second idea about affiliations that they call production interdependencies. In their economic models, they show relationships between production firms as a matrix of coefficients denominated by production prices. The bigger an individual coefficient in the matrix, the stronger the potential relationship, or "dependency" of the firms to produce a good.

One goal of the CEO for finding potential investors is to use the coefficients in the matrix in conjunction with economic statistical methods to help "reveal" and anticipate where the potential investors may be on the internet, so that the marketing message can find them.

Very often, the most common sense ideas on where to find investors are not accurate. The potential interests and relationships tend to be hidden, or unanticipated.

David Bryce and Sidney Winter, in their 2006, work titled "A General Inter-Industry Relatedness Index," (Working Papers for Economic Studies, U.S. Census Bureau) described one application of the statistical technique.

One example they used hidden relationships involved an unexpected relationship between users of batteries and users of razor blades.

Ed Feser used a different statistical technique on a regional input output matrix to develop "clusters" of companies that s technology in common. (Regional Cluster Analysis with Interindustry Benchmarks Edward Feser, University of Illinois at Urbana Champaign, Henry Renski, University of Massachusetts at Amherst, Jun Koo, Korea University, 2009).

Affiliates are similar to members of a supply chain or like intermediate producers in an industrial cluster in the sense that the firms share some common financial or economic interest. In many cases, the affiliates do not know of the potential relationship. The internet marketing strategy is to use the statistical methods to "reveal" the relationship by using code words or code language to alert the Internet user.

The use of the term "affiliates" in this economic relationship application is different than the commonly accepted usage by web firms who also use the term "affiliate marketing." In their usage, affiliate marketing is a type of performance-based marketing in which a business visitor or customer is brought about by the affiliate's own marketing efforts.

An affiliate CrowdFunding marketing strategy is part of a Search Engine Optmization (SEO) marketing plan where a set of terms and phrases are targeted to specific web pages so that when a user searches for one of those phrases, that website will rank on the top of the results.

The CEO of the company that is raising capital uses the search phrases, or keywords, to help the potential affiliates find the company website. The measurement of success of the SEO strategy for a CrowdFunding project is based on the number of visitors that the keywords that drive or attract to the company website.

The CEO is aware that a potential affiliate has two primary financial reasons to be interested in the company. Either the affiliate is potentially interested in the company to get a product to the market, or the affiliate has some financial interest in the company.

The SEO affiliate strategy involves a combination of traditional public relations and marketing, and the newer advertising ranking for the company website on search engines like Google.

The diagram below describes how a marketing strategy to reach these two types of affiliate markets would be work.

Diagram 14 . The CrowdFunding SEO Affiliate Marketing Strategy. ©
2014.

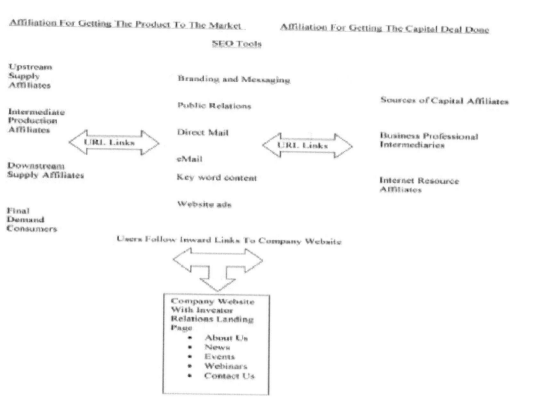

After the potential affiliate has landed on the company Investor Relations
page, the page content must be optimized so that they can access the
information and verify that the company has potential as an affiliate. In
other words, the user begins their investigation of the potential relationship
with the company in order to determine if the company "fits" into the
individual welfare function of the user.

Unlike the individual welfare function that describes behavior of a potential
affiliate, the affinity user is searching on the internet to find resources that
promotes the user's image of the good society. This type of marketing can
be categorized as Social Media Marketing, (SMM), to distinguish it from
Search Engine Optimization (SEO).

The CEO in a CrowdFunding project would use social media marketing to reveal the hidden common interests between the affinity users, who are searching the internet for relationships with other like-minded users who would not generally be aware that the company represents a user that contributes to the user's conception of the good society.

By helping the affinity user imagine the relationship with the company, the CEO can lead the user to follow the inward navigational links the company's website.
Diagram 14, below, describes how the affinity part of the Social Media Marketing Strategy for a CrowdFunding website would work.

Diagram 15. Affinity Social Media Marketing.

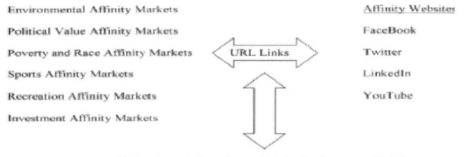

Finding investors means using SEO and SMM in conjunction with internet tools, like a company website, and other websites, where potential investors may be seeking information. The major task of the CEO for finding investors is to combine the tools into a coherent marketing strategy, and then have enough time to manage the marketing strategy and still run the company.

Chapter 8. How To Manage The Rule 506c Offering

Both SEO affiliate marketing tools and SMM affinity marketing techniques must be combined with traditional public relations tools to help internet users find the company. The CEO must manage seven essential marketing tasks all at the same time and also find time for making public speeches and giving webinars about the company.

As noted earlier, the best idea for managing a CrowdFunding project is to begin preparation about six months prior to the start of the project. One benefit of CrowdFunding is that the major time burden in the older venture capital model of negotiating with each individual investor during the period of the offering is replaced in CrowdFunding with an internet platform that allows investors to investigate a predetermined set of terms and conditions, and decide on their own if they like the deal.

This time-saving benefit comes with the cost of the CEO having to do more work upfront, in preparing the entire set of documents for the offering, and building in time to manage the marketing of the CrowdFunding project.

Diagram 16. The Seven CEO Marketing Tasks of Managing The Accredited Investor CrowdFunding Project

1. Push marketing of invitation emails to pre-selected affiliates whose contact information was derived from company data files on suppliers and customers. The push marketing email campaign would invite the email recipient to "learn more" about the company, and would not contain a solicitation to make an investment. The main idea is to alert the recipient to a new opportunity of having a relationship with the company.
2. The creation and management of the company investor relations webpage, that acts as the landing page for inward-bound viewers from external websites. When the potential investor first lands on the page, the mental image of how the company "fits" with the viewer's interests, either affiliation or affinity, must be apparent to the viewer.
3. Preparation and distribution of pull marketing tools, like internet press release distribution, news story distribution, and company announcements must contain the navigation link to the company website landing page.
4. The preparation of strategic pull marketing tools, like placement of ads on angel investor or venture capital matching websites, or other media sites, where investors are using key words to search for information.
5. The preparation and distribution of pull marketing tools, like events

on business calendar websites to attract both affiliates and affinity users who may be interested in the event, and who would follow the link back to the company website.

6. Integration and coordination of the company landing page with the company due diligence portal, where the CEO communicates with potential investors as they conduct their self-guided due diligence of the investment opportunity.

7. Company presentations, either online, or at events, or as a guest on internet television news channels, such as the Private Capital News Network.

In terms of understanding the tasks, the CEO must recognize how the internet has changed everything about raising private capital. Part of that understanding is related to seeing the internet in the historical context of a technological innovation in media communications.

Generally, technological innovations begin in very small niche markets when a tiny group of risk-taking consumers decide to try out a product or service they have never seen before. The internet, as a technological

innovation, allows the CEO to identify the very small niche market of potential investors more efficiently than the earlier methods of communication.

This explanation of the internet as a communications innovation for raising capital via CrowdFunding is relevant. A CEO engaged in CrowdFunding is searching for a very small niche market, but the success of using the internet to find the investors for the CrowdFunding project is very uncertain.

Most of the success of a technological innovation is a market phenomena, when new customers decide to buy the new product, and not a technological or scientific engineering break-through phenomena. The same is true for the success of CrowdFunding using the internet.

Funding success on the internet is mostly related to an extensive marketing campaign conducted by the CEO for a very specific set of potential investors.

The internet and CrowdFunding (the two new technologies) have bred a third new technological innovation called CrowdFunding public relations. The internet presentations and public relations, however, do not transmit the moral value of trust in the same way that a live, in-person presentation does. This is one important factor in understanding how the internet changed the process of raising capital.

Trust is faith that reciprocity will occur in the future, extended in the absence of any evidence. Trust is generated and transmitted in face-to-face communications.

Prior to CrowdFunding, in the older venture capital model, building trust generally meant that the investor extended faith that the CEO would reward the investor in the future. No matter how many lawyers and government agents were involved, the future repayment was always based on an act of trust between the investor and the company, made at the very beginning of the exchange.

The act of building trust was one important reason why venture capitalists and angels placed such a big priority on face-to-face presentations. The venture capitalists would always say that the management integrity of the new venture was the most important factor in their decision to invest. What they meant was that the issue of trust in the integrity of management was important to the investors obtaining their reward in the future.

In other words, the trust exchange is a precursor condition that happens before the capital investment exchange. Nothing about internet CrowdFunding has changed this part of human behavior in private capital market relationships between investors and companies.

The important point for the CEO managing the CrowdFunding process is to recognize that internet marketing must be supported by live presentations, and that the internet presentations, like webinars, must also replicate live presentations.

One of the most interesting parts about trust and capital markets is that both only extend about 50 miles, in a geographical envelope of trust. In other words, in the old days, before the JOBS Act, most companies would raise capital from investors located within the 50-mile envelope of trust.

The 50-mile envelope for both trust and capital is related to tacit, or in-person, communications before and after a capital market exchange. Before the exchange, in the older model, the investor needed to "see" the CEO in person to determine the "trustworthiness" of the CEO. After the exchange, the investor needed to be able to easily drive to the company to observe and verify the ongoing trustworthiness of the investment.

In the new way of CrowdFunding, trust is still essential. But webinars and other internet online presentations, like appearing on a television news program, extend the envelope of trust to a much wider market of potential investors.

If the investor is not able to easily drive to the company, before or after the exchange, then the CEO must use the internet to continuously communicate with the investor to replicate the creation of trust that occurred in the earlier in-person presentations.

In order for trust to be exchanged, the webinar technological platform must replicate the conditions of exchange that investors are accustomed to experiencing in the older model. In the older model, the investors at a presentation would coolly sit back in the audience and assess the presentation made by the company CEO, thinking all the while, "Can I trust this guy to reciprocate?"

In the newer method, the investors still look at the video or computer screen, for tacit clues or small voice inflections, to determine if the CEO and other company presenters can be trusted. But, the investors are searching for clues by watching the webinar presenters on a computer video screen.

In order to gain trust in a capital market webinar, the CEO needs a technological platform that conveys, as much as possible, the rich full details of personal tacit communication.

The viewers need to see and hear the voice of the presenters with crystal clear tone. So much of tacit communication involves voice inflections and tone. The quality of sound must be matched to the ease of accessing the sound because complicated technological interfaces tend to raise suspicions about the authenticity of the presentation.

The best approach for authentic sound is a single VOIP web conferencing technology that does not require the viewers to have the video on one platform and then call in on telephone on another platform.

If the presentation is 100% web based then no telephone will be required. The viewers simply put on a high quality headset, or turn on speakers, to hear the presentation.

While both live and archived videos are important, in live presentations, viewers need to determine if the movements and images seem believable. In other words, in the new method, live video conferencing is the preferred technological feature because viewers need to see the behavior of real people, not scripted actors

The company presenters need to have many graphic tools and exhibits available for the viewers to see during the presentation.

This is actually a big advantage for the technology of webinars over the older in-person presentations because the viewers can see the screen better, and can make copies of the slides or exhibits for later viewing. Most CEOs are accustomed to making slide presentations, like PowerPoint, or putting financial data on PDF pages to show to investors.

The accuracy and crispness of high quality graphics in a live video webinar presentation tend to convey trust.

The company presenters need to be able to switch back and forth between their live presentation to high quality HD videos that support the presentation message. The company videos can be archived on websites, like YouTube, or on the company's own website, so that pass word authorized viewers can go back and review the video after the webinar concludes.

During the live presentation, the videos being shown need to have automated synchronization for those who arrive late or have been distracted during the presentation and need to catch up with the rest of the crowd.

One of the most important elements of establishing trust occurs in the brief exchanges between viewers and presenters. Social media tools are effective in facilitating this type of exchange. The other participants get a chance to see how the executive handles questions and interaction with the audience, which tends to help the viewers gauge trustworthiness.

Technological features like shared white boards, in real time, replicates the older method of audience participation, which tends to facilitate peer mutuality, a value related to reciprocity.

The viewers need to be able to co-browse on different websites during the presentation to check and verify, on their own bookmarked pages, the material and data being delivered by the CEO. In addition, the CEO needs the ability to push web pages to everyone for a dynamic follow-me web presentation so that viewers can bookmark new pages to return to after the presentation.

After the presentation, viewers need to be able to go back and watch it again. It is essential for establishing trust that potential investors can go back and answer the questions that arise after the presentation and web seminar recording software allows the company the ability to archive the presentation video for future viewing.

The video should be easily accessed on any Windows, Mac or mobile device because the CEO does not know when that nagging doubt in the mind of an investor may arise, and when it does, the investor needs to immediately confirm and verify their doubts.

As an important part of the CrowdFunding strategy, the internet material needs to be accompanied by mobile applications for easy access and downloads on all types of internet-connected mobile devices.

In a CrowdFunding project, the CEO needs to manage and control who has authority to view the presentations, which means that the webinar platform needs to have a meeting invitation and registration function. Viewers and guests who register to attend a live internet presentation, or to view an archived presentation, would obtain a user name and password for attending future meetings or company presentations.

This easy future access to data and information would tend to heighten the bonds of trust that an investor may have for making an investment.

Part of this management task is related to a new regulatory burden placed upon the CEO in a Reg D Rule 506(c) related to confirming the credentials of potential investors, 60 days before they actually make an investment. By establishing a management system for controlling the access to information about the company, the CEO is creating the documentary evidence of how the verification of the investors credentials had been established.

One of the interesting characteristics of creating trust is that once trust is initially established, the bonds of trust extend over time, and then extend over geographic distance. The bonds of trust, after initially being established, are generally only broken as a result of some catastrophic betrayal.

This means that the initial capital raise for the CEO will probably occur within the 50-mile envelope of trust, and that after the offering period ends, far-away investors who attended internet presentations and webinars, and decided to invest, will likely remain loyal to the company. The CEO must build into the management system ways of continually communicating with the investors so that if future company events become unpredictable and uncertain, that those events do no lead the investor to the suspicion of betrayal.

As the initial investors leave the location, and move around to different locations, the CEO will want to schedule periodic internet presentations in order to continue to communicate with the investors to keep the bonds of trust strong.

At the very beginning of the offering period, the CEO will need to manage an email campaign to two important target groups of potential investors. The first group of potential investors have some financial reason or interest in the success of the company because they either sell products to the company, or they buy products from the company.

This affinity group is comprised of a contact list of potential investors compiled from the rolodex and contact lists of all sales and support staff in the company. The message of the email is that the company is on an expansion path, and would like to inform the email recipient about the future prospects and plans of the company.

The CEO would invite the recipient to learn more by following the url link back to the company investor relations page.

The second important group of potential investors are the individuals with some latent pre-existing reason for liking the company. Generally, the contact list for this group would be compiled from the professional associations and trade groups of the senior executives of the company, or from internet contacts who communicated with the company.

The message of the email is that the CEO knew of their prior interest, and wanted to invite them to learn more about the company by following the link to the investor relations page.

The email message would not contain any news or information about raising capital.

After the potential investors lands on the company IR page, the CEO must manage social media relations with the potential investors, and that task takes time. The CEO must build into the daily tasks enough time to respond to inquiries and promote the relationship with the potential investor.

Another time consuming management task is managing the linkages and correspondence on social media sites, like Twitter. As in the case with the email message, the task of social media is to convey the idea that the company is in a growth phase and developing new ideas. The CEO would invite the social media viewers to follow the links back to the company IR page, and solicit the viewer's opinions and comments about the company.

Both the email campaign and the social media campaign must be coordinated with a more traditional public relations media campaign that involves issuing press releases and obtaining news coverage of the company.

Each contact with the press and public media must contain a uniform message about the company, and all staff and senior executives of the company should have training in the content and purpose of the company public relations message.

For example, when the CEO schedules a speech or a public presentation, the company would issue a press release about the event, and place the date of the event on internet event calendars. The event becomes a type of focal point for the press and media. The CEO is generating news about the company, and the news is being distributed to both traditional media outlets and to internet distribution centers.

Part of the crossover from traditional public relations to internet social media involves the placement of traditional advertising and marketing on websites that may cater to potential investors that are either affiliates in the supply chain, or affinity viewers who are seeking information. The creation of the ad content, and the placement and distribution of the ads is a strategic and costly task for the CEO.

Each ad and marketing message must contain metrics and performance goals to assess the viability of the ad that the CEO uses to determine the effectiveness of the campaign.

For example, if the CEO placed an ad on an angel investor website, where potential investors seek news and information about investment opportunities, the CEO would want to build in a feedback loop to assess the effectiveness of the ad on the website.

After the offering period ends, it is important for the CEO to remove all the ads and marketing messages from internet websites. The task of removing media from the internet is timely and costly, and complicated. Part of the complications involve internet fraud and hacking of the company media content, and part to the management task of the CEO is to build in internet security measures to protect the company's reputation, prior to, and months after, distributing or placing media content on the internet.

The goal of the internet ad campaign is to solicit interest in the company by inviting users to follow the links to the company IR page. The main idea is to have all potential investors land on the company IR page to begin their self-guided investigation of the company. To the extent that the company website can monitor and track potential investor interest by documenting the user's visit to the website, the CEO would be in a better position to subsequently ask the investor when and how they became interested in the company.

The next phase of managing the CrowdFunding project is for the CEO to invite potential investors to visit the outside accredited investor CrowdFunding website. In the chronology of events for managing a CrowdFunding project, the first phase involves attracting potential investors to the company investor relations webpage.

In the second phase, potential investors follow the url links from the company website to the external CrowdFunding website, as those described in Chapter 3, where the potential investor conducts self-guided due diligence.

One big difference for the CEO to understand about managing a CrowdFunding project is that each investor has their own pace and style of investigating the company and all the investors will be at different stages of investigation, at any moment in time.

Generally, the entire period for investor investigation will be around six months, with an important 60-day period at the end when the investor makes a decision to invest. At that point, the CEO must confirm the investor's identity and credentials, prior to allowing the capital to be transferred to the company account.

The verification and confirmation of the investor's credentials has a shelf life of 60 days. The documentation for verification should probably be kept for the duration of the statute of limitations involving claims of fraud, from either disgruntled investors, or government regulatory agents.

The CEO will need a website user tracking tool on the CrowdFunding website to monitor and track the investor's status and progress in due diligence, and must build into the daily tasks enough time to respond to inquiries and requests from potential investors.

Unlike the older business model of raising capital, in CrowdFunding all investors must be able to see and confirm for themselves, the accuracy and legitimacy of the CEO's responses, which means that whatever the CEO says to one investor must be available for review by all investors.

Routine and ordinary requests for information probably can be handled by the CEO directly. More detailed inquiries will probably need the review of the outside company securities attorney, before the CEO makes the response available on the CrowdFunding website. The response will need to be archived on the CrowdFunding website, under the Frequently Asked Questions page, for the authorized, pass-word protected users to see.

The communication between the CEO and the outside securities attorney will require management time and money. After the response has been posted, it is important for the CEO not to vary from the posted response, otherwise the CEO would not be treating all potential investors uniformly and fairly.

As a part of the work with the outside securities attorney, the CEO would prepare the entire set of offering documents related to the project. The documents would include the form of securities to be issued, such as preferred stock, bonds, and certificates of revenue participation.

This decision about the form of securities is probably the most important decision about the future of the company. If the CEO intends to manage a very profitable business, for an indefinite period of time, then some form of debt would most likely be issued.

For revenue-rich companies, some form of certificates of revenue participation, would be issued.

For CEOs who intend to sell the company within 3 years, some form of convertible stock would be issued.

The issue of the form of securities to issue is related to the risks and legal issues associated with raising capital. According to both Federal securities laws, and most state securities laws, almost anything of value exchanged between an investor and a company is considered to be a security, and any form of communication is
considered to be an offer.

Chapter 9. The CEO's Essential Tools for Managing A 506c Offering

The advice given in this book is aimed at CEOs of small private technology companies and executives in commercial real estate firms who need to raise capital to fund company growth. The capital raise project requires pre-planning, beginning about 6 months before the actual raise begins. The offering period will be about 6 months, and the post-offering period will take another 3 months to settle the transaction.

The best place to begin getting the company ready for the capital raise is on a global website that aggregates data about all websites. The global websites are an essential tool for teaching the language used in the global CrowdFunding community, so that the CEO learns the difference between the types of services that are relevant to the project.

For example, the out-of-business CrowdSourcing website called the entire universe of CrowdFunding by the broad generic term, "crowdsourcing." Under the broad generic term, they categorized 5 major topics of CrowdFunding, including their term for idea gathering from the crowd called "crowdsourcing."

They also included another topic, not related to capital, called the "sharing economy," which is loosely tied to cooperation by businesses around the world.

It is essential information for the CEO to learn the language being used by media and users of websites that describe crowdfunding. A CEO would want to survey and investigate the websites under all the categories in order to begin the selection process of choosing an accredited investor website to partner with on managing the raise.

A CEO would want to investigate the services and costs of the providers to begin the process of selecting the right providers to assist the CEO in the offering.

The most essential outside service provider for the CEO contemplating a capital raise is a securities attorney. On many websites, securities attorneys advertise their services.

A CEO contemplating a CrowdFunding project would want to read the entire set of articles written by potential attorneys before beginning the offering period. The CEO would want to take notes on the articles to categorize and classify the range of issues that an outside attorney must provide to the CEO.

Many of the articles by attorneys are also published on another website called Practical Law, a Thomson Reuters company. Under one of the Practical Law navigation buttons for practice areas is an area titled "Capital Markets and Securities."

Once the CEO opens the guest member account for Practical Law, the CEO would begin to investigate all of the articles under Reg D Rule 506, and also under another topic, called "CrowdFunding."

The free guest membership on Practical Law expires in a short period of time, so the CEO is advised to hurry through the article investigation, looking for both content about CrowdFunding, and also looking for potential lawyers to retain, who may have written an article the CEO likes.

Many of the articles on Practical Law refer to the SEC website for citations to law and regulations. A CEO contemplating an accredited investor CrowdFunding project would want to follow all the links from each Practical Law article to the relevant section on the SEC website, and take notes on what the SEC documents state about CrowdFunding, and especially their documents related to Reg D Rule 506c.

Each state regulates and licenses lawyers. All the lawyers in a particular state form professional associations that are broken down into professional practice areas. The professional associations are different than the state licensing boards, but the names of both organizations are often very similar.

For example, in North Carolina, the licensing board that issues licenses to practice law is called the North Carolina State Bar. The voluntary professional association is called The State Bar Association.

The State Bar is the state agency responsible for regulating the practice of law in North Carolina. The State Bar publishes the North Carolina State Bar Journal, which has articles related to the practice of securities laws in North Carolina.

A CEO contemplating a CrowdFunding project would want to go to the relevant State Bar website and look for articles in the State Bar Journal about CrowdFunding and private offerings, and begin preparing a list of law firms that offer services in the area of securities law and regulations.

The professional association of lawyers in North Carolina is called The North Carolina Bar Association. The Association was founded in 1899, and is a voluntary organization of lawyers, paralegals and law students dedicated to serving the public and the legal profession.

Members of the Association form membership committees in each professional practice area, including the practice of securities law. The committees on securities law break into more defined areas, including the practice related to private offerings.

For example, in North Carolina, the Association provides a referral service, classified by practice area, defined by the internal committee structure that references private placements.

A CEO contemplating a CrowdFunding project would want to investigate the relevant Association in their state, and begin preparing a list of potential law firms that could provide advice and guidance on the capital raise.

The CEO would want to solicit advice and opinions from friends and associates, including other lawyers, about the law firms on the list to begin the process of interviewing firms to represent the CEO's interests.

One reason why the CEO needs to begin preparing the project six months in advance of the offering period is that the selection of the attorney, including the interview process, takes time. The CEO would need to prepare a detailed list of the services to be provided by that attorney for the capital raise before beginning the interview process, and be certain that each law firm provides a full explanation of the services and professional fees.

Selecting the right attorney is the most important task of the CEO, and the project cannot begin until the CEO has a signed letter of engagement from the law firm on the scope of representation and the terms of payment for the services.

The attorney selected will have her own set of business relationships with other outside advisors, including the financial and accounting professionals who may be involved, depending on the size of the offering and the rules selected for the exemptions.

The CEO would want to have prepared in advance, a list of potential outside business professionals that the securities attorney could review, in order to put together the team of outside advisors for the offering.

A CEO contemplating a CrowdFunding project needs a set of internet software tools designed to manage the project. Part of the pre-project planning for the CEO is deciding which set of software tools fits with the type of project that meets the company's needs for capital.

The choice of software needs to be coordinated with the advice and counsel of the securities attorney because the software is often specific to a unique exemption in the law, and the CEO would not want to buy the wrong type of software.

One broad category of software tools is related to marketplace websites that connect the company website to an internet marketplace of buyers and sellers of private securities. The type of marketplace tool is different than the CrowdFunding websites and portals reviewed in Chapter 5 that dealt with the management of the capital raise project.

As an example of a marketplace tool, the CEO would want to investigate both services offered by a software company called CommunityLeader. After the investigation of CommunityLeader, the CEO would take the main words and text from their website and conduct an internet search for other competitor companies that offer this same type of software.

CommunityLeader offers both its main software for helping a CEO manage a project, and also offers a second software product that allows broker/dealers to add a CrowdFunding component to their existing line of business.

This second product is called Apicista. A CEO would not want to confuse the software for broker/dealers with the software for CEOs, although this product delineation on their website is not very clear. It is very useful, however, for the CEO to investigate the service offerings for the broker/dealers because many of the accredited investor CrowdFunding websites reviewed in Chapter 5 offer similar broker/dealer services.

If the CEO ends up selecting a broker/dealer CrowdFunding website to manage the offering, the website should offer the minimum set of services provided by Apicista to broker/dealers.

The entire set of software services offered by CommunityLeader have three applications that together create a compliance-focused platform for marketing and promoting a CrowdFunding project:
- CampaignLeader is a business development platform for companies seeking to effectively develop, implement and support a successful CrowdFunding campaign;
- CommunityInvestor is a smart-phone enabled application for individuals to track, commit and subscribe to the business they want to support; and
- Apicista is a standalone accredited CrowdFunding platform for broker/dealers to connect quality businesses with qualified investors in their own communities.

A review of the services will arm the CEO with the knowledge needed to make a better decision on selecting the right accredited investor CrowdFunding website. The review will also be helpful to the securities attorney in screening and evaluating all the services for regulatory compliance with the exemption selected for the capital project.

The key words and terms used on the websites should be plugged into search engines to find competitors to CommunityLeader.

The CEO would want to create a spreadsheet with all of the benefits and costs of each website, and then call the website CEO to begin discussions about their services. The telephone call is an essential step in the process of getting ready to raise capital because it indicates what the response will be in the future, if the CEO gets in trouble and needs help from the website.

Some websites have very elegant functionality, but very thin support, and the CEO would want to avoid websites that can not respond to website malfunctions.

As an additional note of disclosure, the author of this book, owns and manages an accredited investor CrowdFunding website, and CEOs would want to conduct an investigation of the credentials and qualifications of the owner of The Private Capital Market, as they would do for any outside professional service provider.

Some of the accredited investor websites reviewed in Chapter 5 offer internal marketing and promotion of the CrowdFunding project, and some of the websites outsource this function to outside social media marketing firms. A good place to begin the investigation of outside internet marketing firms is a website based in Southern Florida called SEO 4 Anyone. (http://www.seo4anyone.com/).

The set of services provided by SEO4Anyone is very similar to the set of marketing services outlined in Chapters 6 and 7 of this book. As was the case with comparing the software of CommunityLeader with other software companies, the CEO would want to copy all the key words and phrases from the SEO4Anyone website to conduct an internet search for competitors.

Selecting the marketing company is the third most important task of the CEO because most of accredited investor CrowdFunding success depends on attracting a large group of potential investors to land on the company investor relations page. The marketing task is the biggest difference between the older venture capital model and the new CrowdFunding model of raising capital.

In the chronology of pre-planning tasks for undertaking an accredited investor CrowdFunding project, the first step is selecting the right attorney, the second step is selecting the right website, and the third step is organizing all of the related advertising and promotion of the company's offering.

As a note of caution to CEOs, it is very important not to begin public announcements about the proposed offering until all of these preliminary tasks have been completed. Recall that there is an odd trigger mechanism in Rule 506c that once selected, the CEO can not go back to 506(b), or rely on the older exemption under Rule 4A(2) of the Securities Act. That odd trigger mechanism gets triggered if the CEO makes premature announcements.

During the offering period, and then during the 3 month settlement period, the CEO must manage and administer the escrow of funds that are intended as capital for the company. This escrow step, and then the subsequent use of the funds by the CEO, is a regulated activity that must be coordinated with both the securities attorney and the bank or financial firm that is holding the escrow account.

A CEO contemplating an accredited investor CrowdFunding project would want to interview banks and financial firms for potential escrow partners. As mentioned in Chapter 10 on legal issues, there is a little noted provision related to a private placement that has not been well integrated into the regulatory framework for Reg D Rule 506c.

The provision relates to the requirement that the CEO approve of the transfer of funds from each investor to the company account, on the day of closing.

To review, under 506c, the CEO must certify and verify the credentials of all potential accredited investors, prior to the transfer of funds. Then, a second step, in an entirely different part of the private placement rules, requires that the CEO affirmatively approve each individual investor's transfer of funds.

Then, after the capital has been legally transferred to the company account, the CEO must use the funds in accordance with the disclosure document or private placement memo. Many of the civil suits against the CEO result from disgruntled investors who suspect that the capital is being used for other purposes.

The CEO would want to build in accountability and transparency on the use of funds to build the defense against a disgruntled investor. One possible way to build the evidence is for the escrow agent to continue to offer services for capital withdraws so as to show a transaction history and track record on the use of funds. In other words, the CEO would keep the initial escrow account open, and convert it to a money market checking account to draw out funds.

Recall that if a disgruntled investor complains to the state securities regulator, and the investigation, the CEO faces the prospect of recission, not just for the disgruntled investor, but for all investors.

The best idea would be for the CEO to find an independent escrow agent to handle the transfer of capital transactions, and then to open a money market checking account, titled to the company. Part of the pre-planning for the CEO is to find the right escrow agent that can handle the entire set of banking functions.

Some of the websites reviewed in Chapter 5 have internal escrow accounts, and the CEO contemplating an accredited investor CrowdFunding project would want to review and take notes on the escrow services offered. The process of escrow funds must be linked to the work of the securities attorney, who issues whatever certificates or documents to the investor related to the security purchased by the investor.

For example, if the CEO issued a preferred stock, then the securities attorney would send the investor a stamped certificate, indicating the rights and use of the preferred stock security. The legend and text on the back of the certificate will contain rules related to how the security is restricted from sale or transfer for a certain period of time.

The timing of the delivery of the certificate by the attorney must be closely coordinated with the work of the escrow agent.

As mentioned above, after the offering period is over, the CEO would want to continue an ongoing stream of communications with investors to keep them fully and fairly informed of the company's progress. This investor relations function is another big difference between the older venture capital model, which placed a premium on keeping everything a secret, and the newer CrowdFunding model.

Because of the new provisions related to public marketing in a Reg D Rule 506c, many potential interested parties will know about the company. The CEO would want to build in the tools to keep the investors who made an investment fully informed, while keeping the private company financial information out of the hands of investors who chose not to make an investment.

At some point of time in the future, when the CEO is ready to raise capital again, the existing set of investors become the prime targets of making a second investment, and the other investors, who did not make an initial investment, become the important secondary targets for the second round.

And, at that point, the CEO can begin the accredited investor CrowdFunding project all over again.

Chapter 10. The Financial Risks and Legal Issues for the CEO and the Company

As mentioned above, just about anything of value exchanged between an investor and a company can be defined as a security, and almost any form of communication between a potential investor and the company can easily be interpreted as an offer.

As defined in various Federal securities laws, a "security" means any note, stock, treasury stock, security future, security-based swap, bond, debenture, evidence of indebtedness, certificate of interest or participation in any profit-sharing agreement, collateral-trust certificate, preorganization certificate or subscription, transferable share, investment contract, voting-trust certificate, certificate of deposit for a security, fractional undivided interest in oil, gas, or other mineral rights, any put, call, straddle, option, or privilege on any security, certificate of deposit, or group or index of securities (including any interest therein or based on the value thereof), or any put, call, straddle, option, or privilege entered into on a national securities exchange relating to foreign currency, or, in general, any interest or instrument commonly known as a "security", or any certificate of interest or participation in, temporary or interim certificate for, receipt for, guarantee of, or warrant or right to subscribe to or purchase, any of the foregoing.

The term "offer to sell", "offer for sale", or "offer" includes every attempt or offer to dispose of, or solicitation of an offer to buy, a security or interest in a security, for value. Any security given or delivered with, or as a bonus on account of, any purchase of securities or *any other thing*, (emphasis added), shall be conclusively presumed to constitute a part of the subject of such purchase and to have been offered and sold for value.

The biggest risk and potential liability with any offer is the risk of making a fraudulent statement or misrepresentation that an investor relies upon in making an investment decision. The law states that it is unlawful, in connection with the offer, sale, or purchase of a security, to employ a device, scheme, or artifice to defraud; to make an untrue statement of material fact; to omit to state a material fact; or to engage in an act, practice, or course of business that operates as a fraud or deceit upon another person.

To summarize, there are two major areas of risk in making a Reg D Rule 506(c) offering. First, there is a risk that the CEO may not follow the rules in making an offer, such as filing Form D, at the Federal SEC level.

Second, there is a risk that the CEO may make a misrepresentation about the company, or about any executives affiliated with the company, or the offering itself.

It is important for the CEO to recognize that a fraudulent statement can be either written or oral, and covers all communications on the internet, including all forms of social media, blogs and emails.

Telling one investor one thing about the offering, and then telling another investor something else, for example, could be a form of making a misleading statement.

A oral or written statement could be considered misleading either because it did not state the facts accurately, or because the statement left out important information that an investor needed to know in order to make an informed decision.

Part of this issue of fraud is related to providing the investors enough information that they can fend for themselves, by relying on the accuracy and truthfulness of the statements made by the CEO.

A statement could be considered misleading if there is an absence or omission of explanations, qualifications or limitations or other statements necessary or appropriate to make the statement not misleading. In other words, when the CEO is discussing the offering, all the known facts and downside risk of loss of the investment must be disclosed, and all investors must be treated uniformly in the distribution of the information.

A statement about the general economic or financial conditions or circumstances could be considered misleading. For example, any representations the CEO may make about past or future investment performance may be misleading because of statements or omissions made involving a material fact, including when:

- portrayals of past income, gain or growth of assets imply net investment results achieved by actual or hypothetical investments that would not be justified under the circumstances;
- representations, express or implied, about future investment performance including: representations as to security of capital and possible gains or expenses;
- representations implying that future gain or income may be inferred based on past performance and portrayals of past performance in a manner that implies gains realized in the past may be repeated in the future.

To summarize, part of the risk for the CEO in conducting a CrowdFunding project is the market risk that the company will not meet its performance goals for sales and profits. If the offering documents contained forward-looking projections of sales and profits, and if potential investors relied on those projections in making a decision to invest, there is a risk that the investor will claim that the CEO misrepresented the future potential of the company, if the projections turn out to be inaccurate.

The consequence for the CEO and the company in making a misrepresentation is that the CEO becomes liable, under Section 12(a), of the Securities Act, which could result in the investors in the private placement rescinding their purchase and recovering their capital from the issuer for one year following completion of the private placement.

In other words, the fraud and misleading statement does not simply apply to the investor who was subjected to the fraud. The misleading statement affects all the investors, and part of the liability for the CEO is that if one investor claims rescission, then the entire offering loses its exemption.

At that point, if the offering loses its exemption, then the offering is considered to be a non-exempt offering that should have been registered in the first place. This would be called an "unregistered offering."

The second major risk, after fraud, is related to a regulatory risk that the CEO did not follow all the rules for issuing securities.

The rules tend to vary depending on the amount of capital raised, and the form of security that the company decided to issue. In the case of Reg D Rule 506c, the company can raise an unlimited amount of capital, subject to the restriction that all of the investors must be accredited.

The new Reg D Rule 506c offerings follow the regulatory history from the Ralston Purina Supreme Court decision that the two most potent protections for accredited investors are their own sophistication—their ability to evaluate the merits and risks of any offering of securities—and the meaningful disclosure of or access to material investment information.

The new 506c rules also follow the 1996 the National Securities Markets Improvement Act (NSMIA), which preempted state authority over the registration of securities offered under Rule 506.

In other words, under an accredited investor CrowdFunding offer, the securities to be issued do not need to be registered and reviewed by every state securities administrator, although a copy of Form D may need to be filed at the state level 15 days prior to the start of the offering period, in that state.

The new 506c rules contain two new provisions that are untested and untried. The first new provision is the burden placed upon the CEO of confirming the credentials of the potential accredited investor.

The second new provision is a two-pronged rule that covers both "Bad Actors," and "Bad Events."

Rule 506 offerings prohibit the involvement of felons or other bad actors, either inside the company, or anywhere along the outside chain of authority for issuing securities. The prohibitions cover both predecessor companies, who may have owned beneficial interests in a prior life of the company, or affiliated companies that may be co-owned by the company or its owners.

Potential bad persons who must be investigated by the CEO, prior to the start of the formal offering period include:
- Directors, executive officers, any other officers participating in the offering, general partners and managing members of the issuer.
- Beneficial owners of 20% or more of the issuer's outstanding voting equity.
- Any promoters connected with the issuer at the time of sale.
- Persons compensated for soliciting investors, as well as the general partners, directors, certain officers and managing members of any compensated solicitor.

The CEO must investigate these potential bad persons to see if they may have been involved in a "bad event." Under the new Rule 506(d), an issuer will be unable to rely on the Rule 506 exemption for an offering if any potential bad person had been involved in a "disqualifying event."

Under Rule 506d, disqualifying events include:
- Criminal convictions within ten years before the proposed offering (or five years, in the case of the issuer, its predecessors and affiliated issuers) or court injunctions or restraining orders within five years before the proposed offering:
- in connection with the purchase or sale of a security;
- in connection with making a false SEC filing; or arising out of the conduct of certain types of financial intermediaries.
- Subject to final orders from state securities, insurance, banking, savings association or credit union regulators or federal banking agencies, the CFTC or the National Credit Union Administration that bar the person from associating with a regulated entity, engaging in the business of securities, insurance or banking, or engaging in savings association or credit union activities.

- Any ongoing litigation, including its current status and litigation counsel's assessment of exposure.

In addition to investigating both potential bad persons who may have had something to do with a bad event, the CEO is required to investigate, and reveal all threatened claims or suspected future suits. If any type of lawsuit is initiated while the company is actively marketing a securities offering, the CEO must reveal the filing and prepare an appropriate response to potential investors.

One final area for the CEO to investigate and disclose involves compliance with applicable governmental regulations and any settlements or other agreements with governmental entities, including reporting obligations.

The areas of government and regulatory concern for the CEO include:
- Tax disputes.
- Securities actions (based on, for example, an illegal unregistered offering).
- Employment discrimination or unsafe working condition claims.
- Environmental matters.

This list of Bad Person rules represents wild political and regulatory over-kill and way too much government involvement in the capital markets. It should be noted, however, that the bad person/bad event/government run-in list covers all private, and public, securities offerings, not just those issued under Reg D Rule 506c.

The best management practice for reducing the risk of either a fraudulent statement or a regulatory mistake is to prepare the entire set of offering documents in advance of the offering, and to conduct as thorough investigation of potential investors as they may be investigating the offering.

The two management procedures work in tandem. In other words, parts of the offering documents would be provided to a potential investor, after the investor had made certain warranties and representations about their credentials and qualifications.

After the investor had confirmed receipt of the first set of documents, and subsequently confirmed that the documents had been read and understood, the investor would be provided more documents.

This series of iterations would continue throughout the offering period, ending within 60 days of the investor making a decision to invest in the company. At that point, the CEO, or a designated outside verification company, could verify the credentials of the investor.

On the day of the closing, before capital changes hands, the CEO must again review the list of potential investors, and authorize the transfer agent bank to transfer the capital to the company account.

One final important note about risks concerns the transition in time from the formal offering period to the time the company begins deploying the capital. During the offering period, and in the written offering documents, the CEO described the use of capital. The potential investors relied upon the CEO about how the company would use the capital.

To reduce risks of fraud and misstatements, the CEO needs to set up on ongoing verification and auditing system to account for how the investment capital had been deployed.

The length of time for a civil or regulatory claim to be valid against the CEO would vary from state to state, but would probably always be longer than the 12 month period for the right of rescission.

The most important legal document to be prepared in advance of the start of the formal offering period is called the private placement memo (PPM). It should be noted that under Reg D Rule 506(c), the preparation and distribution of the PPM is not required. In other words, a CEO could possibly conduct an accredited investor CrowdFunding project without creating a PPM.

The PPM serves as an important tool for reducing the risk for the CEO of making a fraudulent statement. The document usually begins with a detailed list of all the many risks and pitfalls an investor would endure by making an investment in the company.

After the CEO had written out all of the risks of the investment, the CEO would always use the document as a reference tool to refer all questions that investors may ask. The investor would review the material in the PPM and then be required to confirm that they had read the material and that the document had answered their concerns.

Generally, the PPM follows a standardized format or template that accredited investors are used to seeing.

The major parts of the PPM are:
- Summary of the offering.
- The risks and suitability of the offering.
- The use of capital from the offering.
- The legal structure of the company, its history, and its certificate of

existence.
- The capitalization of the company and information about current stock and bond holders of the company.
- A description of the company management, company products, business plan, organizational chart, and historical financial data.
- The subscription process.

As noted in an earlier chapter, the presentation of audited financial statements is not required by the rules, but could possibly be an important method of reducing the risk of misstatement.

The PPM should probably include the recent balance statements, prepared according to acceptable accounting practices. A potential investor who inquired further about the statements or had questions, would probably be answered in the Frequently Asked Question part of the accredited investor pass word protected portal, so that all authorized investors could see the information, at the same time.

The disclosure and communications ability of the accredited investor website, used in conjunction with the company's own website, provides a good mechanism for compliance with rules and avoiding fraudulent statements.

The CEO, and the executives involved with managing the CrowdFunding project would be instructed not to make ad hoc oral statements, or issue emails, to potential investors who made inquiries about the offering.

As a part of reducing risk, the CEO would want every potential investor to first register and confirm their credentials on an independent website, that was specifically designed for that company. In other words, websites which aggregate multiple investors, who have the ability, based upon prior registration, to see data and information about an offering, without prior authorization from the CEO, are probably not beneficial to the CEO in reducing risk.

Economists have a concept called the "opportunity cost" of capital that is relevant for the discussion of raising CrowdFunding capital. Part of the idea of opportunity cost is the lost opportunity, or what economists call the foregone or foreclosed opportunities, of alternatives that could possibly have been chosen.

In other words, once a choice has been made about how to raise capital, the other options are gone, or are foreclosed. The total cost of the alternative chosen can be compared to the alternatives not taken, in order to assess the economic benefits of all the alternatives.

CrowdFunding represents a new way of raising capital, and is an alternative to the older method of the venture capital/angel model. In the older model, CEOs would go to an individual venture capital firm and seek capital. The venture firm would set the terms and conditions for investing in the company.

Often, in the older model, the entrepreneur or owner would not meet the performance metrics set by the venture capitalist investors. The investors would then terminate the investment and the company would generally go out of business. The older method had a very high opportunity cost, compared to CrowdFunding, not just in the cash outlay, but in the ultimate survival of the enterprise.

The older model was suited to very early stage companies that had a defined exit path for the investors to take a capital gain. Most venture capital firms were not interested in established operational companies because those companies did not have a defined exit path for the investors, and generally the amount of capital needed by the company was too small to attract the attention of investors.

In CrowdFunding, the total cost of capital is lower, but comes with defined upfront out-of-pocket cash expenditures for the CEO that are not payable by the company in the older model because the investors are paying some of the upfront costs. The costs of capital in CrowdFunding can be categorized as the upfront costs to execute and manage the CrowdFunding project, and the interest rate on the capital that is sufficient to attract investors.

The interest rate is sometimes called the price of capital. From the financial perspective of the potential investor, the opportunity cost of investing in a company with an interest rate of 8% when a nearby investment offers 10% is the lost opportunity of 2%.

From the perspective of the CEO, the opportunity cost of issuing capital at a 10% interest rate, compared to 8%, is a lost opportunity to obtain cheaper capital.

In most CrowdFunding projects for established companies, the form of securities issued will be some type of interest bearing security, like a convertible bond, that features both an interest rate, and an opportunity for capital gain, if the company is bought or goes public.

Most established companies have stable top line revenues from product sales, and the CEO uses part of this revenue to pay the interest and principle on the bonds.

If the company is bought, the investor would convert the bond to stock, and then sell the stock as a part of the transaction, for a capital gain.

An attractive rate of interest on a convertible bond for a private technology company would be around 12% to 16%. In other words, it would cost the CEO about 12% in interest payments to obtain capital. The CEO would be obligated to pay the rate of interest, and pay the principal on the bond, so that at the end of the term of the bond, the investor had obtained a return of both interest and principal.

For example, on a $1,000,000 CrowdFunding raise, at a rate of interest of 12%, it would cost about $120,000 in interest payments. Generally, the length of time, or term, for a corporate bond would be around 10 years, so there would be 120 interest payments, at about $1000 per month.

The principle repayment would be about $8,333 per month, for a total payment of about $9,333. The CEO would need to be sure, before embarking on the capital raise, that the estimated monthly revenues of the company were adequate for making the monthly payments.

A simple rule of thumb would be that the investment of capital in the company would generate an internal rate of return for the company greater than 12%, otherwise the opportunity cost of the capital is greater than the expected rate of return.

There are not many variables available for the CEO to manage to lower the interest rate on capital. Generally, the rate of interest is set by competitive market forces that the CEO confronts upon entering the capital market. One way to influence the cost of capital is for the CEO to engage in marketing and promotion to create competitive bidding for the securities, so that the capital has the lowest competitive rate of interest possible, given the market conditions when the CEO enters the market.

Marketing and promotion costs to gain a competitive rate of interest are the biggest out-of-pocket costs for the CEO for CrowdFunding, followed by the legal costs for preparing the offering documents and the costs associated with following the rules and regulations.

Assuming that the average hourly fee of a securities attorney is $150, the tasks associated with the legal work for an accredited investor CrowdFunding project could be assigned to each task.

Diagram 15 outlines the legal tasks, organized by the chronology of events that usually take place in managing a private offering. For example, the 10 hours of legal work to prepare the terms of the offering would be preceded by many hours of prior discussion with the attorney about the terms. So, the actual billable hours, shown in the Diagram as 10 hours, could actually be much higher, if the attorney is adding on the prior discussion time to the time that the documents are being drafted.

One important idea for the CEO in managing the open-ended upward fee for legal work is to give this diagram, or something like this diagram of tasks, to the attorney before the legal fee meter begins to run.

The CEO would want the attorney to include the set of tasks to be performed, and the manner that discussion times are billed, into the attorney's letter of engagement to avoid surprise and dismay, when the attorney's first bill arrives.

Part of the attorney's work cannot be estimated at the beginning of the engagement, such as the time it takes to respond to an investor, or the time to prepare a uniform response for all investors.

The best idea is to provide some threshold amount of time, and have the attorney agree that if the billable hours for the task goes over the threshold, that a new estimate would be made on the fees for that part of the engagement.

Diagram 15 is only intended to provide an estimate of the upfront, out-of-pocket costs the CEO may encounter for issuing securities. The Diagram does not address what happens if there is a subsequent regulatory problem or a civil complaint against the CEO.

That contingency should be addressed in the letter of engagement, calling for a second letter of engagement to handle that subsequent need for legal representation.

The new method of CrowdFunding requires that the CEO have a sufficient amount of cash to begin the capital raise. As a rough estimate, the CEO should have about $30,000 in the company bank account before the raise begins.

Diagram 17. The Securities Attorney's List of Tasks For An Accredited Investor Offering

Task	Hours Per Task	Estimated Fee
Drafts Term Sheet, Private Placement Memo and Subscription documents.	10	1500
Conducts legal due diligence on company for compliance with securities rules and Bad Boy laws.	10	1500
Files Form D and obtains Blue-Sky state registration approval, if it is required.	5	750
Files documents and forms related to public solicitation in a Reg D Rule 506(c) offering.	5	750
Reviews the text and language in all public documents related to the offering, including the business plan, and power point presentations, and marketing materials and coordinates that language with the legal requirements of all offering documents.	5	750
Drafts NASAA Attorney's Opinion Letter for posting on password protected web page.	2	300
Advises corporation on how to make uniform and fair responses to inquiries from potential	10	1500
Reviews all responses for "Frequently Asked Questions" for full disclosure and fairness.	10	1500
Receives and reviews all subscription documents from potential investors.	5	750
Prepares and mails stock certificates to investors after the date of closing.	3	450
Total legal fees		$9750

The legal work needs to be coordinated with the tax and accounting work of the Certified Public Accountant to prepare financial documents and to review the accuracy of financial projections, including the reasonableness of the assumptions used by the CEO in making any projections.

Assuming that the average hourly fee of the CPA is $150, the estimated fee for the tax and accounting work can be estimated.

Diagram 18. List of Tasks for the CPA for an Accredited Investor CrowdFunding Project

Task	Hours per Task	Estimated Fee
Prepares, when required, the audited financial statements for inclusion in the business plan and private placement memo, in accordance with SEC regulations of a Reg D private offering.	10	1500
Assists client in preparation of future revenue projections for use in power point presentations and business plan documents.	10	1500
Prepares valuation of company for posting on the website in the business plan and Term Sheet, using standardized, uniform methodology that will be replicated annually in on-going financial reporting to investors, if required by securities regulations.	5	750
Prepares semi-annual reviews and annual audited statements of income, balance sheet and cash for placement on the investor relations portal on the company web site, after the offering ends.	10	1500
Assisting the CEO and the legal counsel in setting the pricing and valuation for the securities that will be issued in the CrowdFunding project.	10	1500
Total tax and accounting fees		$6750

Generally, the fixed minimum legal and tax costs for a CEO in a CrowdFunding project would be around $15,000, no matter the amount of capital raised. In other words, there is a type of fixed cost to conduct an offering, just to open up the Reg D window, no matter the amount of capital raised. It costs just as much to do a $1 million raise, as it would cost for a $5 million raise, because the work is about the same.

This cost is not the same between a public offering, like an IPO, and a Reg D private offering.

For comparison, the legal and accounting costs for a public offering of $25,000,000 would probably be about $750,000 to $1.5 million, for a comparable list of tasks to issue securities on the public market. In other words, while the list of tasks is about the same for the attorney and CPA for a private versus a public offering, the professional costs go up with the amount of capital raised in a public offering.

As mentioned above, one approach to lowering the costs of capital is to promote competition among potential investors and bankers. Marketing and promotional costs for an internet-based CrowdFunding project could vary between a minimum of $4000 to as much as $20,000, depending on the level of services required by the company to attract potential investors.

The table below lists the major items of expenses for marketing and promotion, with cost estimates provided, as a way of providing rough guesses for each item.

Diagram 19. Marketing and Promotional Costs for Accredited Investor CrowdFunding

Paid 15 minute light talk advertorials produced by company and delivered to an internet social media website.	$4,500
Paid 15 minute light talk advertorials produced by professional studio company delivered to an internet social media website..	$6,000
Archived company 30 min webinar video taped by professional studio for internet social media website.	$3,000
Archived company power point produced by company delivered to an internet social media website..	$1,000
Archived company power point produced by professional media company delivered to an internet social media website..	$1,500
Banner ads displayed for 30 days on outside	$500
Video Ad insertion into Webinar (live & archived) 2,000 viewers per client.	CPM per 1000

	$15
Video Ad Pre-roll on PPT with 2000 viewers	CPM per 1000 $12
Corporate sponsorship of live internet tv program.	$15,000
Paid 15 minute light talk advertorials produced by company and delivered broadcast ready on internet tv channel.	$2,500
Paid 15 minute light talk advertorials produced by professional studio company for broadcast distribution on internet tv channel.	$3,500
Live webinar for broadcast distribution on internet tv channel.	$3,500
Push marketing of invitation emails to 1000 pre-selected affiliates whose contact information was derived from company data files on suppliers and customers.	$1500
The creation, hosting and management of the company investor relations webpage for 6 months	$1200
Preparation and distribution of pull marketing tools, like internet press release distribution, news story distribution, and company.	$1500
The preparation of strategic pull marketing tools, like placement of ads on angel investor or venture capital matching websites, or other media sites, where investors are using key words to search for	$1500
Third party verification of accredited investor status 25 investors.	$1250

The cost to create and produce a video can be combined with the costs to broadcast the ad on the internet television channel, or the more traditional cable or broadcast television channels. The television ads and promotions would need to be coordinated both with the company's own investor relations web page, and on outside social media websites, such as those described in Chapter 5.

A staff person inside the company that is raising capital would be responsible for managing the marketing and promotion of the accredited investor CrowdFunding project, and that cost would need to be budgeted by the CEO for at least 6 months. The main goal of this staff person is to use social media and promotion to drive potential investors, first to the company website, and from the company website, to the CrowdFunding portal website.

An important point to remember from Chapter 5, on accredited investor CrowdFunding websites, is that many of the sites do not allow the CEO to conduct independent marketing and promotion. This type of prohibition tends to eliminate the benefits of CrowdFunding for the company, and places the company in a dependency relationship on the website to do adequate marketing, similar to the dependency of the company created by the older venture capital model of raising capital.

The CEO has an opportunity cost that is not a cash outflow but affects the operation of the company. Every hour that the CEO spends on the capital raise project represents an opportunity cost of not managing the operations of the company.

During the CrowdFunding project, the CEO will be giving speeches and making presentations that will detract from the time that the CEO can perform routine management tasks.

The personal appearances by the CEO are essential for building trust with potential investors, and nothing about internet marketing changes this essential task of the CEO for building trust.

One reason why the accredited investor CrowdFunding websites described in Chapter 5 are essential as a management tool for the CEO is that the websites reduce the amount of time the CEO spends on the capital raise. In accredited investor CrowdFunding, the functionality of the website allows potential investors to conduct their own self-guided due diligence, at their own pace.

In the older, venture capital model, the CEO would spend a considerable amount of time attempting to negotiate the terms of the deal with multiple sources of capital. The website acts to substitute the CEO's personal time spent on managing the capital raise for the functionality of the investor conducting the self-guided investigation, and allowing the CEO to respond to questions in a uniform and consistent manner for the benefit of all potential investors.

As described in Chapter 5, all of the existing CrowdFunding websites have a cost to use them. Generally, in the case of the FINRA broker-dealer CrowdFunding websites, the cost of using the website is a percentage of the capital raised. For example, a website that charges a fee of 5% of the capital raised on a $1 million raise would charge a fee of about $50,000.

In that broker-dealer model, the total amount of capital raised from investors is paid to the broker-dealer's account, and the broker-dealer deducts the fee, before transferring the capital to the account of the company.

To take the earlier example of a $1 million raise, at a 12% rate of interest, the $50,000 broker dealer fee would be added to the $120,000 interest payment, for a total cost of $170,000 for conducting the CrowdFunding project with the broker-dealer. The full cost of the capital project would then add up to around $200,000, with the addition of the legal and marketing costs, paid directly by the company.

It is important to recall from Chapter 5 that some of the websites have a minimum threshold trigger mechanism related to the amount of capital raised. Under the threshold model, if the amount sought by the company is not successful, then the website returns all of the capital back to the investors, and the company gets no capital.

This tends to create a very high opportunity cost, of an all-or-nothing gamble for the company.

The costs of using the CrowdFunding website must be included in the CEO's projection of costs for the capital raise. Some of the websites include the new cost of third party verification of the potential investors in their fees, and some of the websites outsource that new cost to independent third parties.

The CEO can also conduct the verification of the investor's credentials on his own volition. The opportunity cost and liability of making a mistake is greater for an in-house verification, however. It is not clear, yet, what the regulatory penalty would be for making a mistake on an investor's credentials, but it would probably fall in the parameters of the costs the company would absorb for a rights of rescission process.

Chapter 12. Your Next Raise: The Future of Accredited Investor CrowdFunding

Often, the growth cycle of a technology company requires additional capital, after an initial round of growth capital has been raised. Generally, the addition of growth capital follows the product innovation cycle of the company, for commercializing a new version of an existing product.

Most product innovations occur in a 3 to 5 year period. Part of the legacy revenues of the older product are used by the CEO to fund the work of product commercialization, but often, the CEO will require a lump sum addition of capital to complete the product commercialization process.

So, about every 3 years, the technology company CEO will be confronted with the task of raising capital, again. Part of the management of the future raise is to re-use parts of the earlier raise, so as not to re-invent the wheel. Another part of the management task is to make the terms and conditions of the future raise consistent and compatible with the earlier raise, so that all investors involved in all of the raises over time are treated fairly.

Part of the benefit of the new CrowdFunding model, and accredited investor CrowdFunding websites, is that the task of future capital raises is less costly because the historical documents of the prior raises are archived on internet websites, for use again.

In addition, if the CEO had opened an on-going investor relations portal to keep investors informed, those earlier investors would be the most likely investors in the subsequent rounds of capital.

As mentioned in Chapter 11 on costs of raising capital, the amount required by established companies is usually around $1 million, which is too small an amount to attract the interests of angel partnerships and venture capitalists. In order to raise $1 million in capital, the out-of-pocket costs for an accredited investor project would be between $15,000 to $30,000.

The CEO should anticipate that there will be changes to the environment of raising capital in the future raise, and begin building in the flexibility in the offering documents to adapt to the future changes.

CrowdFunding was an important improvement for filling the capital gap confronted by established technology companies for obtaining small lump sums of growth capital. Seen in an evolutionary perspective, CrowdFunding can be interpreted as the appearance of a new species in the capital market environment, and as a new species, it is likely that CrowdFunding will evolve into new variations.

It is also likely that the emergence of CrowdFunding will cause other, unexpected, innovations in capital markets. Among the possible future innovations would be private secondary markets, such as The SecondMarket, that allows early investors to trade their shares, similar to the exchange of securities in the public markets.

As they say on their website, "We're enabling companies to provide liquidity, raise capital and communicate with key stakeholders through products that give control to companies, not to Wall Street. We're changing the market, so entrepreneurs can change the world."

The SecondMarket was created in 2004, and is registered with the SEC as an alternative trading system, which means that it is authorized to provide a market mechanism to trade private securities. Trading private securities is what they mean when they say that they are providing liquidity for private shareholders of private companies.

The connection between accredited investor CrowdFunding and The SecondMarket is addressed on their website under a new section called "investor solicitation." As they state, "SecondMarket, a FINRA registered broker-dealer, takes on the administrative burden and heightened regulatory requirements related to accreditation verification so companies and funds can focus on their capital raise."

In other words, SecondMarket offers an integrated set of services related to making a market for private securities. They provide services to issue private securities, comply with CrowdFunding rules, and to trade securities among investors, after the required holding period has been met.

The SecondMarket represents a type of capital market infrastructure for private investments that has not previously existed. In other words, from an evolutionary perspective, the emergence of CrowdFunding caused a related species to emerge that offers a type of food for CrowdFunding. This new infrastructure can be expected to continue to evolve.

Just a small glimpse of the future can be seen in a type of organizational support structure that offers clearing and custody services for private securities offerings to facilitate more exchanges. For example, Clearing and Settlement is a new type of internet service that helps buyers and sellers of securities to help manage financial commitments.

Their website is a hybrid between an auction site, and a transactions clearing marketplace. Integrated within their website is an information exchange system where website members may post Indications of Interest (IOI) for privately negotiated transactions in a wide variety of assets. Website members may post an IOI of public or private securities, business opportunities and business assets.

A CEO contemplating an accredited investor CrowdFunding raise would want to carefully survey the market of clearing and custody firms for the exchange, and form relationships today that could be useful for the future raise.

The reason this step is important is that an independent market exchange platform provides useful price information about exchanges that may occur between today and the future raise.

This price information tends to make the future valuation of the future raise more objective.

It is also likely that competitors to SecondMarket will emerge that provide similar services related CrowdFunding. Among the likely new services will be market platforms that function like closed end mutual funds in technology specific sectors, and regional private equity markets that provide services for companies in specific metro regions.

In this case, the securities of one company that is listed on the SecondMarket, would be combined with other companies, and the entire package of companies would trade on the SecondMarket, similar to how the shares of closed end funds trade in the public markets.

A CEO contemplating a CrowdFunding project should build in language in the offering documents that anticipate these likely future developments. Part of the accommodation to unknown future changes is the addition of terms that provide enough flexibility for the securities to be traded in private markets, and to be converted to public shares, if that opportunity arises in the future.

Another likely development in capital markets is new forms of private securities that trade in their own markets, such as the TigrCubs, the revenue participation security that trades in the alternative trading system established by Entrex. The connection between CrowdFunding and Entrex is that an established technology company, with stable top line revenues, could issue TigrCubs in a CrowdFunding project, and then have those securities available for trading in the Entrex market.

The emergence of TigrCubs points to a likely development in CrowdFunding where TigrCubs, from a single company, are aggregated into a bigger pool of TigrCubs, and the entire pool of TigrCubs is traded among much bigger investment banks.

The bigger institutional investment banks would not be interested in a single company, but would be attracted to a much bigger pool of TigrCubs. The key factor that makes TigrCubs attractive for aggregating into bigger pools is the common terms and conditions for all TigrCubs.

The bigger investment banks have greater confidence in the quality and content of the underlying securities in each pool, and it is the common terms and conditions which provides this level of confidence for future trading on Entrex.

The pools of TigrCubs have the appearance of being like a closed end sector-specific mutual fund. In other words, TigrCubs with specific investment performance criteria, like secure interest payments, can be grouped together, and investment banks that desired that specific set of criteria would be attracted to buy that pool of TigrCubs.

Just like the SecondMarket will likely have competitors in the future, it is likely that Entrex will have competitors. Entrex is only 3 years old, and has made considerable progress in creating its alternative trading system. The securities offered under the Entrex platform provide an attractive alternative to issuing equity ownership shares for companies that are not going to have a future exit event, and do not want outside owners participating in the management decisions of the company.

A CEO contemplating either a CrowdFunding project today, or a future raise, would want to investigate the entire market for future developments related to new forms of revenue participating securities, like TigrCubs.

One of the reasons that the JOBS Act of 2012, obtained widespread political support concerned the recognition by elected leaders of the connection between private capital investments and national economic growth. This relationship between capital markets and economic growth is likely to spur more policy linkages between regional economic development and CrowdFunding.

In the future, it is likely that there will be regional private equity mutual funds that target investments directly to small technology companies within the regional economy, and the creation of regional stock exchanges for both private and public companies, similar in concept to the Toronto Stock Exchange, and the Toronto Venture Exchange, for small companies. Companies usually raise private capital on the junior exchange, and then "graduate" to the senior exchange when they go public.

A glimpse of how future CrowdFunding may be different than current CrowdFunding can be gleaned from analysis of the provisions in the JOBS Act that do not deal directly with Title II CrowdFunding, but could be compatible with future CrowdFunding projects. This analysis does not include Title III, commonly known as non-accredited investor" CrowdFunding.

The other provisions of the JOBS Act are reviewed below:

Title I of the JOBS Act is commonly called the IPO On-Ramp for 'Emerging Growth Companies,' (EGC). An EGC is defined as a company with less than $1 billion in revenues over the past fiscal year.

The law provides two major benefits to a company that is raising capital as an EGC. First, an EGC that is potentially on the On-Ramp would be exempt from being required to make certain costly and burdensome filings and SEC disclosures related to the IPO rules.

Most of the exemptions deal with certain financial and accounting disclosures, including the new Dodd-Frank requirement of executive compensation. As reported by an analysis by Practical Law Company, while the ECGs that are filing under the On-Ramp provisions seek certain benefits, the primary anticipated results of nonfinancial disclosure are not being observed because the companies have decided to continue to make these disclosures.

The survey revealed that all of these EGCs included a full three years of financial statements, with only approximately one-fifth including less than five years of Selected Financial Data. Surprisingly, only one quarter of the EGCs availed themselves of the reduced executive compensation disclosure requirements contemplated in Title I.
An EGC is also permitted to file a confidential IPO registration statement with the SEC that must be made public at least 21 days before it begins actively promoting the sale of its offering, and can 'test the waters' with certain qualified buyers to gauge interest in the offering.

"Testing the waters" in this quasi public offering is somewhat related to the advertising and solicitation rules for a Reg D Rule 506(c) private offering. A CEO contemplating an accredited investor capital raise would want to build in transitional language from the advertising and solicitation of the private offering to the possible future public offering that "tests the waters" for the IPO.

The big difference between the accredited investor capital raise and the Title I On-Ramp is the intervention of investment bankers and underwriters in the IPO process. Even with the reduced reporting requirements, the On-Ramp IPO will be more costly to the company than the accredited investor CrowdFunding process, under Title II.

There is nothing that requires, however, a company to retain outside investment bankers and underwriters to issue securities, and one important future development will be the use of the private offering process to issue public securities.

In other words, the IPO process followed by Google, which was called the Dutch Auction, will likely emerge as a more important part of the transition from private securities to public securities, under Title I of the JOBS Act.

A CEO contemplating an accredited investor CrowdFunding project today would want to build in flexibility in the language of the offering documents to accommodate a possible future Dutch Auction to the public markets, as provided for under Title I.

Title IV of the JOBS Act made modifications to an existing rule under Section 501 called Regulation A. The reason for the modification concerned the relative obscurity and non-functionality of the rules under the older Reg A.

The old Regulation A permitted the sale of $5 million of securities to both accredited and unaccredited investors so long as the issuer filed an abbreviated registration statement with the SEC. The company was burdened by the onerous task of filing documents with state securities administrators, some of which were critiqued, in each state where funds are solicited for compliance with relevant state law requirements

The new provisions under Title IV are called Reg A+. The new Reg A increases the offering limit from $5 million to $50 million in a 12-month period. The process of issuing securities seems to be similar and compatible with the provisions of Title I. However, the exact wording of the rules for Reg A+ has not been finalized yet, by the staff of the SEC.

A CEO contemplating an accredited investor CrowdFunding project would want to continually monitor developments on the rules for the new Reg A to provide flexibility for combining a current private offering with a future Reg A+ offering.

The new Reg A+ exempts companies from the burdensom state registrations would not be required, although state securities regulators are actively opposing this part of the new law. One reason for the delay in issuing final rules on Reg A+ is related to this political opposition by the state regulators.

In addition to the state registration exemption, the new Reg A allows securities to be immediately tradeable, without the current one year holding period. This feature allows a CEO even greater opportunities for providing liquidity, especially if the securities are issued on an alternative trading system, like SecondMarket.

The rules on reselling private securities are related to another provision called Rule 144. Under the older law, securities sold under Rule 144A are deemed to be restricted securities and cannot be freely resold to the public without registration or an exemption (Rule 144(a)(3), 1933 Securities Act).

Without the guidance of specific written rules, large investment banks carved out a practice that allowed a large bank, called a Qualified Institutional Buyer (QIB), to enter into a prior agreement with a private company to buy all the shares of the private offering, and then to immediately turn around and sell the ostensibly restricted securities to other large banks.

In other words, the large banks figured out a way around senseless regulations on re-selling securities, in order to trade restricted securities.

Generally speaking QIBs are institutions that own or invest on a discretionary basis at least $100 million of securities and are considered to be sophisticated investors. No individual accredited investor qualifies for QIB status. In other words, the definition of a "sophisticated" investor is different than the definition of an "accredited" investor.

It is likely that the provisions of Reg A+ will be changed to accommodate new procedures that allow QIBs to continue their current 144 A trading practices, and CEOs would want to discuss this potential development with their securities attorney prior to starting either a Reg A+ or a Title II CrowdFunding project.

Another feature of the new Reg A is a very similar provision of "testing the water" like Title I. To summarize this part of the new law, Title I, Title II, and Title IV, all have new provisions related to public solicitation and marketing of a securities offering. A CEO would want to consider how to combine all of these provisions to gain maximum exposure to the potential investors who may have an interest in the offering.

The decision about how to market an offering is related to where the CEO wants to take the company in the future. Under a certain set of circumstances, the CEO may build in flexibility to take the company public in a modified IPO. Under another set of circumstances, a CEO may build in flexibility to sell the company to a bigger competitor or to an investment banking firm.

Alternatively, the CEO may decide to conduct a second accredited investor CrowdFunding campaign.

The main idea is that the future environment for raising capital will be different than the current environment, and the type of capital required in the future depends on what kind of company the CEO wants to grow.

The final portion of the JOBS Act is Title V, and it raises the threshold on the number of shareholders a company can have before it is subject to 1934 Exchange Act annual reporting requirements.

Previously, under the older provisions, a private company could remain private until it reached 500 shareholders. Title V changes this limit to 2,000 shareholders, or 500 shareholders who are unaccredited.

As preciously mentioned, the advice in this book relates to only accredited investor CrowdFunding, and generally advises a CEO against accepting capital from any non-accredited investor because of the increased regulatory burdens associated with non-accredited investors.

Just as the case that the future environment for raising capital will be different, another part of evolutionary economic theory suggests that the future regulatory burdens related to non-accredited investors will become more burdensome. Once a certain regulatory path has been chosen, it tends to become entrenched in the environment.

About the author: Laurie Thomas Vass

Laurie Thomas Vass is a regional economist and a registered investment advisor representative of Investment Management & Insurance Advisors, Inc., a North Carolina registered investment advisory firm.
As an independent investment advisor to real estate companies and technology companies, Vass has been providing investment advice to CEOs on private placements since 1988.
Vass is a professional money manager, and is the inventor and holder of a research method patent on selecting technology stocks for investment.
She was cited by Peter Tanous, in The Wealth Equation, as one of the top 100 private money managers in the nation.
Vass is the author of seven books.
She has published over 90 scholarly articles on the Social Science Research Network author platform, and is currently ranked in the top 1.4% of over 330,000 economic authors, worldwide, on the SSRN platform.
Vass is a graduate of the University of North Carolina at Chapel Hill and has a undergraduate degree in Political Science and a Masters degree in Regional Planning.
In addition to being a licensed investment advisor, Vass is also licensed in North Carolina as a property, casualty, life and health insurance agent, and is a North Carolina real estate broker.
Prior to starting her advisory company in 1987, Vass was a regional economist and advisor to the Board of Directors of B. C. Hydro, and also served as an economic advisor to the N. C. Commissioner of Labor. She learned the retail stock trade as a broker, at E. F. Hutton.
ltv@privatecapitalmarket.com

Made in the USA
Middletown, DE
27 April 2021